To Michael and Fran
   Enjoy your reading of
Kohelet and I wish you many
years of confronting it.
               Benjamin Segal
               Feb. 2017

KOHELET'S PURSUIT OF TRUTH
A New Reading of Ecclesiastes

KOHELET'S
Pursuit of
TRUTH

A New Reading of
ECCLESIASTES

Benjamin J. Segal

Jerusalem 2016

מכון שכטר למדעי היהדות
Schechter Institute of Jewish Studies

gefen גפן
publishing house בית הוצאה לאור
JERUSALEM ◆ NEW YORK   Est. 1981

Cover Design: Leah Ben Avraham/Noonim Graphics
Typesetting: Raphaël Freeman, Renana Typesetting

ISBN: 978-965-229-892-8

1 3 5 7 9 8 6 4 2

Schechter Institute of Jewish Studies
4 Avraham Granot Street
Jerusalem Israel 91160
972-747-800-600
Books@schechter.ac.il
www.schechter.edu

The Schechter Institutes INC.
Box #3566
POB 8500
Philadelphia, PA 19178
1-866-830-3321
schechter@thelapingroup.com

Gefen Publishing House Ltd.
6 Hatzvi Street
Jerusalem 94386, Israel
972-2-538-0247
orders@gefenpublishing.com

Gefen Books
11 Edison Place
Springfield, NJ 07081
516-593-1234
orders@gefenpublishing.com

www.gefenpublishing.com

Printed in Israel

* * *

Library of Congress Cataloging-in-Publication Data
Names: Segal, Benjamin J., author.
Title: Kohelet's pursuit of truth : a new reading of Ecclesiastes / Benjamin
J. Segal.
Other titles: Bible. Ecclesiastes. 2016. | Bible. Ecclesiastes. English.
Segal. 2016.
Description: Jerusalem : Gefen Publishing House Ltd., [2016 = 5776] |
Includes bibliographical references. | Text of Ecclesiastes in Hebrew with
English translation; commentary in English.
Identifiers: LCCN 2016033432 | ISBN 9789652298928
Subjects: LCSH: Bible. Ecclesiastes--Commentaries.
Classification: LCC BS1475.53 .S44 2016 | DDC 223/.8077--dc23 LC
record available at https://lccn.loc.gov/2016033432

Publication of

KOHELET'S SEARCH FOR TRUTH:
A New Reading of Ecclesiastes

was made possible through the generosity of

The Morris & Beverly Baker Foundation

Rabbi Gary & Laya Charlestein

Charles Dimston & family

Rabbi Elliot & Marlynn Dorff

Mark & Adele Lieberman

Claudio & Penny Pincus

Robert & Arleen Rifkind

Paul & Sheri Robbins

Mary & Saul Sanders

Ken & Andrea Saffir

Ed & Barbara Zinbarg

Set your shoulder joyously to the world's wheel: you may spare yourself some unhappiness if, beforehand, you slip the Book of Ecclesiastes beneath your arm.

Havelock Ellis, The New Spirit

All the clearly unsystematic existentialist philosophies, such as those which we encounter in the pages of Nietzsche, Dostoevsky, Kierkegaard, Camus, Tolstoy...are, as far as I am concerned, an ongoing series of footnotes to the thought of Ecclesiastes.

Haim Shapira, Ecclesiastes: The Biblical Philosopher [in Hebrew]

King Solomon made a great mistake in seeking wisdom. The more a man is sensitive and wise, the more he suffers in his life.

Anton Chekhov, Notebook, 1921

He [Kohelet, the speaker] is at one and the same time the examiner and the examined, the student and the teacher, the dream and its interpretation.

Zali Gurevitch, Kohelet's Account [in Hebrew]

A book is a mirror.

Georg Christoph Lichtenberg, Notebook, 1795–1796

Contents

Kohelet's Words Part III
Death and Enjoyment (11:9–12:7)

The Narrator, Looking Back
An Epilogue (12:8–14)

Review Essays and Further Thoughts

Preface

How rare it is that a work of literature endures as a living challenge for more than two thousand years! Ecclesiastes is one such volume, short but hugely impactful on both heart and mind. How beautifully ironic that the book that bequeathed the statement, "There is nothing new under the sun" to the world has confronted every generation anew across more than two millennia.

Is it time alone, then, that justifies this, an additional interpretation of Ecclesiastes? Oddly enough it is precisely the plethora of interpretations, from the distant and the more recent past, that cries out for a reassessment. The range of overviews is daunting, from one commentary that labels this book the essence of skepticism to another that calls it the essence of piety. One interpreter writes "Qoheleth [the name of the book's speaker, variously transliterated] loved life," whereas another summarizes the book as saying: "Life is profitless, totally absurd." One emphasizes "utter existential despair," another, "acceptance and joy." One article epitomizes "the pessimism of Kohelet" and another "the optimism of Kohelet."[a]

Such disparities call out for some sense of order. I propose that there is, in fact, a discernible direction within Ecclesiastes, a story of questioning and change. I claim that we have erred in seeking answers from a book that presents questions, seeking a full philosophy in a narrative tale, and seeking consistency where there is development.

That said, I clarify my vast debt to commentators of the past. Whatever appears here is but a small addition to their works and could never have been written without them. In particular, I acknowledge the late Prof. Robert Gordis, one of the twentieth-century's premier commentators on Ecclesiastes,

a. For an extensive and detailed review of approaches see Ingram, pp. 44–49, including the noted quotations.

with whom I first studied the book many years ago. Although at times I disagree with him, the interest and fascination he left with me are reflected throughout.

Beyond that, added commentaries are always in order. In that regard, it is worth citing the rabbinic midrash[a] interpreting Ecclesiastes 1:7 – "All the rivers go to the sea," meaning that all man's wisdom goes to his heart, "but the sea is never full," meaning that the heart is never full.

I also extend my appreciation to the leadership of the Schechter Institute of Jewish Studies and to the staff of Gefen Publishing. Further, on a global basis, I wish to thank the many who have participated in my classes on Ecclesiastes. Every session became a learning experience for me. The same holds true for the many who shared their reactions to ideas, sections, and chapters. Rabbi Dr. Harvey Meirovich of the Schechter Rabbinical Seminary in Jerusalem reviewed an earlier version of the manuscript and helped me clarify my presentation. I am in particular debt to two outstanding Bible scholars – Prof. Shalom Paul of the Hebrew University and Dr. George Savran of the Schechter Institute of Jewish Studies – who helped me with their enthusiasm and their critical comments on the entire volume. Evelyn Grossberg, my manuscript editor, again sharpened both my thinking and my articulation, and I am profoundly thankful for that.

I am most proud and honored to have this book associated with individuals and groups who have a long-standing record for support of Jewish scholarship. I am proud to call them both supporters and friends. Their names appear at the beginning of this volume. May they merit many more years of accomplishment.

Above all, I thank my wife, Judy. Kohelet advises: "Experience life with a woman you love…, for that is your portion in life" (9:9). I have been so blessed. Her love and support make all possible.

Finally, this volume is dedicated to my siblings, Leslie, David, and Susie, not only in admiration for all they have accomplished in their different fields, but also for the many moments of inspiration, insight, encouragement, and understanding across all these years.

Benjamin J. Segal

Jerusalem, 2016

a. *Kohelet Rabbah* 1:16.

Brief Introduction

In this section, I briefly introduce Ecclesiastes and the principles that guided this translation and commentary. A full explanation of matters touched upon here can be found in the Review Essays that follow the text and commentary. (For those who prefer, it is possible to read those essays first.)

An Exceptional Book

Troubling, puzzling, fascinating, and challenging, Ecclesiastes is unlike any other book in the Bible. It is a tale of a failed search for certain knowledge. The narrator who presents the book summarizes "everything" with an intense phrase: "Vapor of vapors," says Kohelet [the name of the quoted speaker] "everything is vapor."

In this book, a man seeks, through experimentation and observation, assured knowledge of what pursuits will bring him benefit. He does not find it, as he learns that the way of the world is beyond the ken of mortal man. Nevertheless, he offers advice as to how to best survive. The fascination, of course, lies in the detail, for which one must read the text. I reflect on that detail in the commentary that accompanies the text and in an extended way in the essays that follow.

Ecclesiastes is in the third section of the Hebrew Bible, "Writings," and is one of several works that are best defined simply as "good literature," varied explorations of human relationships to the world and to God. It is a self-declared work of imagination. It cannot be pigeon-holed as one specific type of literature. Indeed, the author takes advantage of several formats.

The language indicates that the text was written in the third century BCE, that is, toward the end of the biblical period. This date begs for comparison with the contemporary Greek schools of philosophy, but it is the consensus of interpreters that no one of them fully parallels, or could be the source of, the conclusions drawn by the speaker, Kohelet. However, most accept the proposition that specific ideas or formulations might have been borrowed.

Ecclesiastes's appeal across the generations is reflected in part by the many phrases that have become well known, such as "vanity of vanities, all is vanity" (1:2), "to everything there is a season and a time to every purpose under heaven" (3:1); "a three-ply cord is not quickly broken" (4:12); "better the end of a matter than its beginning" (7:8); "there is nothing better under the sun than for a man to eat, to drink, and to be merry" (8:15); "the race is not won by the swift, nor is the battle won by the strong" (9:11); "cast your bread upon the waters, for after many days you shall find it" (11:1); "rejoice, young man, in the days of your youth" (11:9); and "of making many books there is no end, and much study is a wearying of the flesh" (12:12).[a] These are but examples of the work's popularity.

Content and Emphases

Ecclesiastes is primarily a first-person account by Kohelet. The text, a retrospective, speaks of his efforts, his failures, his reactions, and his advice, all enclosed in a tale reflecting on his personal history.

Over and above a division into units and sections, which allow the reader to progress comfortably, there is a wonderful sweep to Kohelet's words, which move from the grandest scale to close observation of others and, finally, to a focus on dying and death. This movement is bolstered by life changes that he experiences as the text moves on.

The story is first presented by a narrator who introduces (and will conclude) the body of the text. The reader will then encounter, sometimes without clear differentiation, varied voices of Kohelet: the poet, the storyteller, the young searcher, the older teacher, and the heir to religious and Wisdom traditions. One is often challenged to distinguish the voice that is being used or which voices are possible candidates for ascription. The "narrator" is another voice, one that sometimes disagrees with Kohelet. Throughout, in the background,

---

a. In this paragraph I cite verses as they are commonly used, not as translated in this commentary. Most English citations evolved from the King James Bible (first edition, 1611).

but not always articulated, are inherited societal values and "truths." Thus what is by framework a story is on another level an ongoing dialogue.

Further challenging the reader is the use of methods that are inherently multivalent or ambivalent (poetry, metaphor), with the added complication in Ecclesiastes of original language and new uses of old terms (for the interpretation of which one cannot depend on biblical precedent).[a]

Ecclesiastes reflects the "knowable" world, where empirical evidence is found (in the words of the text, "under the sun"). It is, in essence, a story, and one should not jump to the conclusion (underlying many commentaries) that the book offers a philosophy or a theology, even if, by raising questions and making suggestions, it is meant to have an influence on one's thinking. Thus the book is very modern, approaching postmodern, for by its nature it empowers the reader. By implication there is an invitation to the reader to relate to the character of the speaker, Kohelet, as a consideration when weighing the messages recorded in his name.

The Present Translation and Commentary

As all commentaries and translations reflect conclusions reached by the interpreter during the long process of study that precedes the actual writing, I begin by noting the conclusions that formed the basis of this interpretation.

This is a "literary" interpretation, but because this ever more popular term covers a range of approaches, I add further clarification. "Literary" here does *not* suggest a resort to or a categorization by present academic (cross-generational) theories regarding the nature of literature. Rather, it implies a tendency to try to let the text speak for itself, on the assumption that form and usage complement content in indicating meaning. Among these are repetition, framing, symbolic language, division into units, and clear references to other parts of the Bible.

Basic to this approach is the understanding that good literature rarely offers an unambiguous or closed line of thought. Rather, it is purposely multivalent and includes options of understanding, which the reader is expected to appreciate. This commentary seeks to make the reader aware

---

a. Some of these terms, one suspects, represent the first efforts in the Hebrew language to deal with terminology and concepts drawn from the Greek philosophical environment.

of these legitimate alternatives. Multivalence does not imply a necessity of choice among meanings – the text may reflect more than one meaning, and the present interpretation is designed to open the reader to this complexity.

"Literary" here also connotes the import of consecutive reading and attention to elements of form and style such as vocabulary, the use of poetry or prose, repetitions, refrains, and so on. However, it does not imply that all the content was originally composed as one consecutive text. The opposite may be the case – the book itself indicates that these are comments collected from across a lifetime, and one encounters, for example, different types of literature in subsections, voices of the speaker at different ages and in different circumstances, and apparent conflicts among sections. That said, the work as a whole demonstrates a pattern of change and progression, testifying to a final work that, while it may have drawn on Kohelet's early statements, was assembled and carefully presented.

I note that I grant initial credence to the received form of the book as a unit, rarely resorting to external explanations of difficulties (as found among commentators who tend to "solve" challenges by removal, after first labeling them as "glosses," "later additions," "corrections," and such). I also grant preference to the Masoretic Hebrew text. (This approach is shared by most modern commentators, but one will find here relatively greater effort to hold to that text.) In particular, I reject efforts to correct the text on the basis of what would seem more "logical" or "consistent" to the commentator.

This translation attempts to reflect the Hebrew original even at the cost of mellifluence. Repeated roots in Hebrew are repeated in English and dissonance between plural subject and singular verbs (and vice versa) is sometimes maintained. One should also note that selections I have deemed to be poetry are indented. Throughout the consecutive commentary, translations of the text from Ecclesiastes appear indented and thus differentiated from the commentary. As this volume is intended for a general readership and because it includes the full Hebrew text for those who wish to consult it, transliterations are chosen only in order to reflect sound with maximal possible consistency.[a] For the same reason, notes appear in two formats – as footnotes (indicated by letters) of clarifications on that page, and research notes (indicated by

a. In most cases, transliteration is based on the American National Standards Institute, Standard Z39.25-1975.

numbers), which focus on more technical references (sources of insights, disagreements with other commentators, and other biblical parallels), which appear together toward the end of the volume. References in notes citing a work only by the author or a brief title refer to sources detailed in the bibliography at the end of this volume.

Terminology

Words remain the first building blocks of literature. Some translations can be controversial. The following terms that appear in this translation and commentary should be noted:

IN THE COMMENTARY

- "Kohelet" is a transliteration of the main speaker's name (which is also the name of the book in Hebrew, although we do *not* use it as such). The root of the name means "gather" and may refer to gathering people or maxims together. The term does not appear anywhere else. (In citing other authors, I maintain their chosen transliterations of this term.)

- "Ecclesiastes," an early attempt to translate "Kohelet" (meaning "one of the gathering"), is the Latin name for the book, taken from the Greek. I always use it as the title of the book as a whole.

- "Author" always refers to the presumed author of the book Ecclesiastes, never to the speaker Kohelet, nor to the "narrator," who introduces and concludes the book.

- "Bible" as used in this commentary refers to the Hebrew Scriptures, the "Old Testament" in the Christian tradition.

TRANSLATIONS

- "Vapor" (*hevel*) is a basic and oft-used metaphor. "Vapor" reflects the word's original denotation, not its connotation (which is "insubstantiality in time and place") nor the varied implications of the metaphor. This term is translated in many versions (including the classical King James Bible) as "vanity" (which reflects the connotations).

- "Anguish" (*re'ut ruach*) is a complex phrase, possibly coined by the author. It consists of two words: the first possibly related to "bad," "break," "pursue" (as a shepherd), "thought," or "desire," and the second to "breath," "wind," or "spirit." I approximate the translations in some ancient versions and medieval commentators.

- "Toil" (*amal*) appears as both a verb and a noun. Even the noun has two possible implications: work and its consequent rewards. When two uses appear in one sentence, I translate the noun as "spoils of toil."

- "Under the sun" (*tachat hashemesh*), a term unique to Ecclesiastes in the Bible, indicates the immediate world, wherein empirical evidence can be found. (Biblical cosmology holds to a universe that also includes the heavens and "above the heavens," where God is often placed.)

- "Good" (*tov*) is closer to "beneficial" (as I sometimes translate) than to "ethically or morally correct."

- "Fail(ure)" (*ch-t-'*) is the opposite of good, that is, not bringing benefit to (a) man. (The Hebrew sometimes implies "sin," as clarified by the context.)

Structure

The commonly accepted division of biblical books into chapters is a late (thirteenth century CE) effort, and at times is not at all helpful. However, no later proposed division of Ecclesiastes into subunits has merited wide acceptance. The following factors define the sections of Ecclesiastes as presented here. Externally, there is an outside frame (comments by the "narrator," beginning and end), within which appear the words of Kohelet (the bulk of the book), in three units.

- Part I, an opening tale ("When I Was a King"), presented within two frames. The outer frame is an assertion that humans cannot achieve advantage for themselves. Within those assertions are two poems describing the world, and enclosed within those poems is the fanciful tale of a king's search through personal experimentation.

- Part II consists of six sections of observation of, and advice to, others, each ending with Kohelet's conclusion that it is best to take advantage of what enjoyment one can find. In each section there is a "core term," a term that appears more there than in any other section.

- Part III is a final poem of old age and death, a tragic balance to the eternity and constancy of the universe that marks the poems of part I.

"Units" (titled "parts," indicated by roman numerals) and "sections" (indicated by arabic numerals) refer to subdivisions as noted above. "Paragraphs" refer to subdivisions of a section. Just as the noted divisions do not appear in the original text, neither do the titles I have added, and they should be considered part of the commentary.

A complementary structure is one of progress, as certain elements change as the book moves forward. These changes are noted in the commentary and summarized in the essays that follow. To allow easy reference to, and comparison with, other commentaries and translations, I indicate the commonly accepted chapter and verse division throughout. "Chapter" and "verse" will always relate to that division.

The Narrator, Looking Forward

An Introduction (1:1–2)

Summarizing Overview

A Bold Foray

א א דִּבְרֵי קֹהֶלֶת בֶּן־דָּוִד מֶלֶךְ בִּירוּשָׁלָ͏ִם:

1 1 The words of Kohelet, son of David, a king in Jerusalem.

The opening verses of Ecclesiastes announce a bold foray into the world of the imagination as a fictive character of royal pedigree and pre-eminent ancestry offers a most decisive yet nearly heretical contention.

KOHELET. The speaker is announced by an otherwise unknown Hebrew name based on the root "gather" (*k-h-l*), with a professional type ending ("gatherer," possibly of crowds or of sayings); hence some translate "teacher" or "preacher," but there is no certainty. Two such forms appear as proper names (or their substitutes), both from the Second Temple period.[a]

SON OF. This can indicate a "descendant of" or a "child of," but the other biblical uses of the phrase (in the singular) with the name "David" refer only to a son, and (see the next paragraph) it seems that the author had Solomon, David's son and heir, in mind as a model (though not a direct historical ascription).[b]

A KING IN JERUSALEM. The author thus confirms that this is to be a fictional autobiography, a genre of literature known from elsewhere in the ancient world. There was no king named Kohelet, and some of the subsequent details do not fit any known king. Indeed, in 1:16 and 2:7, 9 Kohelet makes reference to all those who preceded him "over [or 'in'] Jerusalem," an inappropriate statement coming from Solomon, for before his father David, the city had not

a. Ezra 2:55–57, Nehemiah 7:58, 60. See Review Essays 4.1A for detail.
b. "Son of David" is used for sons other than Solomon (II Sam. 13:1 and II Chron. 11:18).

been in Israelite control. However, the persona is clearly based on Solomon, son of David and Israel's third king, who was known for both wisdom and for wealth, these attributes being basic to what is said of Kohelet in chapters 1 and 2.[1]

THE WORDS OF. This same phrase opens the biblical books of Jeremiah and Amos.[a] The reader expects an anthology or a collection, possibly of wide retrospective scope.

$$\text{א:ב הֲבֵל הֲבָלִים אָמַר קֹהֶלֶת הֲבֵל הֲבָלִים הַכֹּל הָבֶל:}$$

1:2 "Vapor of vapors," said Kohelet, "vapor of vapors; everything is vapor."[b]

Ecclesiastes begins (and ends[c] – see 12:8) with this external summarizing overview (by the narrator). Henceforth, the text (until 12:8, with the exception of two words in 7:27) will be the words of Kohelet.

No English can do justice to the reverberating insistence of the Hebrew, which uses five repetitions of a single term (if we equate singular and plural) of a total of eight words in the sentence. No other biblical repetition is so intense. In addition, two other words, "Kohelet" and "everything" (hakol), echo each other, and these two are partial echoes of "vapor" (hevel) through the h and l sounds.

The phrase is shocking to the ancient Hebrew ear. "Vapor of vapors" is a superlative[d] formulation (like "Song of Songs," "King of kings," "Holy of Holies," and so on). In all biblical uses but one, the extreme referenced is something positive. Here the superlative is reversed, indicating a negative, ultimate physical and temporal insubstantiality,[e] since "vapor" is something that is most fleeting and impossible to hold.

"Vapor" is repeated throughout the book, but there is another kind of

---

a. As well as Proverbs 30:1; 31:1.

b. For full explication on the translation "vapor," see Review Essays 4.1B.

c. Thus it is a classic *inclusio*, a framing term that indicates a (or the) major theme of a work.

d. The absence of a definite article in this instance leads some to rank this as "exceptionally vaporous," rather than "maximally vaporous."

e. Other biblical superlative subjects include God, Lord, heaven, and beauty. The one negative is "slave of slaves" (Gen. 9:25), which shares the lack of the definite article only with vapor.

echo foreshadowed as well. A threefold repetition in one verse is one of the book's stylistic characteristics – see 1:6; 3:19, 20; 7:28; 8:8, 14, 17; and 9:6 (respectively, "turning," "destiny," "everything," "find," "no," "there is [are]," "find," and "even their").[2]

The format of stating the first word(s) of a quotation, then indicating the speaker and then repeating the first words with the rest of the sentence is a known literary flourish, one that is also found in Psalms 124:1 and 129:1.

"Said" is in the perfect mode, which can be translated into past or present tense ("says") in English. Here I opt for the past in light of the end of the book, which clarifies that this opening is spoken by the one presenting the book, evidently speaking after Kohelet is dead.

The first two sentences thus form a classically effective literary opening. Its striking assertion, the mystery of what lies behind it, the intriguing name,[a] and the combination of ancient king with an extremely negative evaluation all serve to entice one to read on.

---

a. If by Ecclesiastes's time, the "Song of Songs [of Solomon]" was already popular in Israel, "Vapor of Vapors" may have been intended as a title of sorts, a wry reflection of a different view of life from that of Solomon in Song of Songs, who, as will be clear from verse 1:12, is the model for the story that is told in chapters 1 and 2.

Kohelet's Words Part 1

My Life as a King (1:3–3:15)

Part I, Section 1

The Song of Wind and Sun (1:3–11)

אַ:ג מַה־יִּתְרוֹן לָאָדָם בְּכָל־עֲמָלוֹ שֶׁיַּעֲמֹל תַּחַת הַשָּׁמֶשׁ: ד דּוֹר הֹלֵךְ וְדוֹר
בָּא וְהָאָרֶץ לְעוֹלָם עֹמָדֶת: ה וְזָרַח הַשֶּׁמֶשׁ וּבָא הַשָּׁמֶשׁ וְאֶל־מְקוֹמ֫וֹ
שׁוֹאֵף זוֹרֵחַ הוּא שָׁם: ו הוֹלֵךְ אֶל־דָּרוֹם וְסוֹבֵב אֶל־צָפוֹן סוֹבֵב | סֹבֵב
הוֹלֵךְ הָרוּחַ וְעַל־סְבִיבֹתָיו שָׁב הָרוּחַ: ז כָּל־הַנְּחָלִים הֹלְכִים אֶל־הַיָּם
וְהַיָּם אֵינֶנּוּ מָלֵא אֶל־מְקוֹם שֶׁהַנְּחָלִים הֹלְכִים שָׁם הֵם שָׁבִים לָלָכֶת:
ח כָּל־הַדְּבָרִים יְגֵעִים לֹא־יוּכַל אִישׁ לְדַבֵּר לֹא־תִשְׂבַּע עַיִן לִרְאוֹת
וְלֹא־תִמָּלֵא אֹזֶן מִשְּׁמֹעַ: ט מַה־שֶּׁהָיָה הוּא שֶׁיִּהְיֶה וּמַה־שֶּׁנַּעֲשָׂה הוּא
שֶׁיֵּעָשֶׂה וְאֵין כָּל־חָדָשׁ תַּחַת הַשָּׁמֶשׁ: י יֵשׁ דָּבָר שֶׁיֹּאמַר רְאֵה־זֶה חָדָשׁ
הוּא כְּבָר הָיָה לְעֹלָמִים אֲשֶׁר הָיָה מִלְּפָנֵנוּ: יא אֵין זִכְרוֹן לָרִאשֹׁנִים וְגַם
לָאַחֲרֹנִים שֶׁיִּהְיוּ לֹא־יִהְיֶה לָהֶם זִכָּרוֹן עִם שֶׁיִּהְיוּ לָאַחֲרֹנָה:

1:3 What advantage can man gain through all the spoils for which he toils[a] under the sun?

> 4 A generation[b] goes and a generation[3] comes,
> but the earth remains forever the same;
> 5 and the sun rises, and the sun sets[c]
> and hastens[d] to the place whereat it rises.
> 6 Going south, turning north, turning,

a. Here (and henceforth) "spoils" is from the same root as "toil" (*amal*), implying "wealth accrued from hard labor." In earlier Hebrew, the root emphasized misery and pain.
b. "Generation" – a time period ("age, era"), corresponding to the poem's focus on non-human elements.
c. "Sets" is an echo in Hebrew; the same term (*ba*) is used as "comes" in the previous verse.
d. Literally, "pants for."

turning goes the wind; and upon its turnings, the wind
  comes back.*a*

7 All the rivers go to the sea,

but the sea is never full; to the place from which the rivers
  go, there they continue to go.*b*

8 All things plod on:[4]

no man can portray,*c*

no eye can totally see,

no ear can fully hear.*d*

9 What was is what will be, and what was done is what will
  be done,

and there is nothing new under the sun.

10 There is a thing of which one might say, "See, this is new" – [but] it
already was from of old; it was before our time. 11 There is no memory
of first ones,*e* and neither will those who will exist later be remembered
by those who will exist there following.

Through a rhetorical question (v. 3), Kohelet opens assertively with the inef-
fectiveness of achieved wealth to change anything and then expands on the
point, first with a striking poem and then with a prose summary. Considered
independently, the poem does not necessarily reflect the preceding rhetorical
question. As placed in the book, verse 3 forces itself upon the succeeding
poem.

The poem, verses 4–7, details constancy in all of creation's four

a. The wind swirls, and the reference to only north and south may be a conventional
summary (cf. Song 4:16), which may in turn be based on their opposition – south winds
in Israel are dry, whereas north winds bring rain.
b. Some prefer "to the place where the rivers go…," emphasizing that the sea does not
fill, rather than the cyclical motion. As translated, implied are underground currents that
return water to the riverheads.
c. "Portray" is literally "speak," a pun, in that "speak" and "things" have the same root, *d-b-r*
(which also means "words"). Indeed, an alternative interpretation of the first phrase is "all
words are weary" (or "wearisome" – see endnote 4). Thus "no man can portray" also hints
at the impossibility of Kohelet's goal of communication, which has been summarized in
verse 1:1 as his "words."
d. Literally, "a man cannot speak [about it], an eye cannot be satiated seeing [it], an ear
cannot be filled hearing [it]." The sense is unending repetition, beyond any person's grasp.
e. Probably people, but possibly actions.

dimensions – time, east–west, north–south, and on and below the surface.*ᵃ*
Several commentators also suggest that the verse includes the four base sub-
stances in Greek tradition – earth, fire, air, and water.[5] The poem brilliantly sets
motion against progress: every detail is constantly on the move, but nothing
changes. The movements vary: ages follow one another, the sun cycles, the
winds are in tumult, and the rivers mysteriously (underground?) reverse their
flow. However, there is an implied uniformity (note the frequent repetition
of terms), and all the motion reflects monotony, with no change.

The point is brought home in verse 8 by a summary ("all things plod on" or
"…are wearisome") followed by three details, each beginning with "no" (in
the Hebrew as well). The absence of objects for "see" and "hear" also reflects
man's inability to comprehend.

Here Kohelet is evidently echoing the Creation story in Genesis 1, using
four basic terms from that account: "earth," "sun," "wind" (in many translations of Genesis, this term rendered "spirit"), and "sea." The Genesis text
imposes order and logic on the world, leading to man's major role. The
opening of Ecclesiastes, while reflecting order, uses the terms for a diametrically opposite effect. Here the physical world remains unchanged, and any
apparent movement simply obscures its essential intransience, whereas the
order of Genesis is the background against which the drama of interaction
will unfold.

Further, in Genesis, man is the pinnacle of creation. In Ecclesiastes, mankind's only role in the opening section is that of a figure too small to grasp the
totality of it all (v. 8). Verse 3 had indicated that nothing that man achieves
will change anything, even for himself. The poem also notes man's inability
to encompass everything, providing a heavy backdrop for the next section in
this unit, the (human) search for what is worthwhile. In summary: Creation
sets the tone in both texts, but in opposite ways.[6]

One should note that the poem, verses 4–7, is much less disheartening
when read alone. In fact, if considered as a separate poem it could be conceived of as a reinforcement of the Genesis narrative, bearing a message of
comfort through regularity. It is the verses around the core poem (3, 8, and

---

a. The rivers were evidently thought to return to their sources beneath the earth's surface
(*NJPS*, citing the Targum and Rashi), a rough equivalent of evaporation (cited by Ibn
Ezra). Note that another biblical term for "river" (*nahar*) also denotes subsurface ocean
currents (cf. Ps. 24:2).

9) that give the text its negative implication. Partially because a second poem (3:1–8) is similarly circumscribed by an added sentence (with 3:9 being nearly identical to 1:3, adjacent to this poem!), one suspects that within the story, the persona Kohelet might have written these core poems earlier, and much more ambiguously,[7] only attaching the specifically negative interpretation to them now, as he arranges his book. The reader is thus immediately alerted to the possibility that Kohelet's outlook will evolve.

Verse 9 returns to the basic element, time, restating the absence of change (also reflected in the two prose verses that follow). Verse 9 closes as did verse 3, with "under the sun," a phrase both exclusionary (not heaven or above) and inclusive (everything else). One should recall that in the original Genesis account, the sun is placed within the sky, which divides the upper waters from the lower. Moreover, many biblical verses place God in the sky (heavens) or above it. The phrase "under the sun" is unique to Kohelet, appearing twenty-five times. (He also uses "under the heavens," found elsewhere, three times.)[8]

There is one further possible implication of Kohelet's denial of anything being new, though it is uncertain – at best a possibility to be considered. The denial that there can be anything "new" might hint at rejection of the Jewish eschatology that flowered around the period of the destruction of the First Temple and the years following. That eschatology often used the word "new," foreseeing a "new thing" (Isa. 43:19; 48:6; Jer. 31:21), a "new heart and new spirit" (Ezek. 18:31), a "new covenant" (Jer. 31:30), and "a new heaven and a new earth" (Isa. 66:22), among others.

Part I, Section 2
Trial and Failure (1:12–2:26)

Here Kohelet begins a long overview of his search for meaning, one that is "pseudo-autobiographical," implying that any reader would know that there had never been a king named Kohelet. In the second unit of the book, he goes on to speak from perspectives that could not possibly be those of a king. The sum of these perceptions indicates either that Kohelet was a king who voluntarily gave up his throne (an unheard of occurrence in antiquity, but reflected in the words "I was a king"[a]) or that this imaginative first tale is a literary work created by the fictive character Kohelet. This character, then, would thus be adopting a ploy sometimes used by ancient authors who would attribute a work to a famous hero, king, etc. (Here a fictive character attributes a tale to himself as a fictive king!)

I divide this section into paragraphs by areas of concentration. In each case (at the start of the first paragraph and near the end of all the subsequent paragraphs), Kohelet uses the term "vapor," a sad conclusion that he has found nothing solid to hang onto. He finally resorts to the insight that appreciating enjoyment when it happens to appear is the best that one can do.

FIRST EXPERIMENT: WISDOM

אֲבֹ אֲנִי קֹהֶלֶת הָיִיתִי מֶלֶךְ עַל־יִשְׂרָאֵל בִּירוּשָׁלָ͏ִם: יג וְנָתַתִּי אֶת־לִבִּי
לִדְרוֹשׁ וְלָתוּר בַּחָכְמָה עַל כָּל־אֲשֶׁר נַעֲשָׂה תַּחַת הַשָּׁמָיִם ׀ עִנְיַן
רָע נָתַן אֱלֹהִים לִבְנֵי הָאָדָם לַעֲנוֹת בּוֹ: יד רָאִיתִי אֶת־כָּל־הַמַּעֲשִׂים
שֶׁנַּעֲשׂוּ תַּחַת הַשָּׁמֶשׁ וְהִנֵּה הַכֹּל הֶבֶל וּרְעוּת רוּחַ: טו מְעֻוָּת לֹא־יוּכַל
לִתְקֹן וְחֶסְרוֹן לֹא־יוּכַל לְהִמָּנוֹת: טז דִּבַּרְתִּי אֲנִי עִם־לִבִּי לֵאמֹר אֲנִי

a. Rashi emphasizes that the term indicates that he is no longer king. The Hebrew could be understood "I have been a king."

הִנֵּה הִגְדַּלְתִּי וְהוֹסַפְתִּי חָכְמָה עַל כָּל־אֲשֶׁר־הָיָה לְפָנַי עַל־יְרוּשָׁלָ͏ִם
וְלִבִּי רָאָה הַרְבֵּה חָכְמָה וָדָעַת: יי וָאֶתְּנָה לִבִּי לָדַעַת חָכְמָה וְדַעַת
הֹלֵלוֹת וְשִׂכְלוּת יָדַעְתִּי שֶׁגַּם־זֶה הוּא רַעְיוֹן רוּחַ: יח כִּי בְּרֹב חָכְמָה
רָב־כָּעַס וְיוֹסִיף דַּעַת יוֹסִיף מַכְאוֹב:

1:12 I, Kohelet, I was a king over Israel in Jerusalem, **13** and I applied my heart to studying and to probing with wisdom all that is done under the heavens – a bad concern that God gave for mankind to be concerned*a* with! **14** I have seen all the deeds done under the sun and behold, everything is vapor and anguish*b*

> **15** a twisted object unfixable,*c*
> and a void immeasurable.

16 I, I spoke with my heart, saying: "I – behold I have increased and accumulated more wisdom than any who preceded me over Jerusalem, and my heart has seen much wisdom and knowledge." **17** And so I led my heart to know wisdom and to know depravity and folly, and I came to know that this too was anguish, **18** for –

> within much wisdom there is much vexation,
> and one who accumulates knowledge accumulates pain.

The phrase "over Israel" limits the conceit of the autobiographical work to the generation of Solomon. After his time, the kingdom split, and a "king over Israel" (the latter name was kept by the northern polity) could not apply to a king in Jerusalem, which was the capital of the south.

In choosing to begin his survey autobiographically, Kohelet is anticipating one possible reaction to all that follows, namely the dismissal of his conclusions as partially reflecting his own limitations. By adopting the visage of the all-rich, all-wise king, he establishes his qualifications – if anyone could test the world, he would be the one.

---

a. "Concerned" – possibly carries a secondary meaning, for the word could mean "afflicted," even though the term is not used that way elsewhere in Ecclesiastes. This is one of the few places where Kohelet seems to criticize God directly.

b. "Anguish." See Review Essays 4.1C.

c. Literally, not able to be "set straight," as in 7:13 and 12:9. Some take verse 15 as a known aphorism, approximately, "That which is twisted cannot be made straight, and [i.e., just as] a void cannot be measured."

This first overview via autobiography begins with a reflection on the process itself, and Kohelet's clear indication that his pursuit of wisdom has led to anguish. Here one also finds a first insight into Kohelet the man through his regret over humanity's inherent drive for truth, and that in the strong terms: "vexation" and "pain." Further, the double uses of "I" and the references to his own heart might hint at loneliness; Kohelet's only partner in dialogue is himself.

This rejection of wisdom in terms of its results seems to be in direct contrast to other statements found in Wisdom literature, which claim that happiness derives from wisdom, such as Proverbs 3:13ff.

SECOND EXPERIMENT: ENJOYMENT

א אָמַ֣רְתִּי אֲנִי֮ בְּלִבִּי֒ לְכָה־נָּ֛א אֲנַסְּכָ֥ה בְשִׂמְחָ֖ה וּרְאֵ֣ה בְט֑וֹב וְהִנֵּ֥ה גַם־ה֖וּא הָֽבֶל׃ ב לִשְׂח֖וֹק אָמַ֣רְתִּי מְהוֹלָ֑ל וּלְשִׂמְחָ֖ה מַה־זֹּ֥ה עֹשָֽׂה׃

2 1 I, I said in my heart, "Come, I will test you through enjoyment;[a] so experience a good life,"[b] and behold, that too is vapor.

2 Of laughter I said, "It is depraved"
and of enjoyment, "What does it accomplish?"

This paragraph may be self-standing or it may be a prelude to the coming experiment with wealth. Kohelet later accepts, and even embraces, enjoyment for its own sake, although he never abandons his rejection of "laughter."

THIRD EXPERIMENT: WEALTH

ג תַּ֣רְתִּי בְלִבִּ֞י לִמְשׁ֤וֹךְ בַּיַּ֙יִן֙ אֶת־בְּשָׂרִ֔י וְלִבִּ֖י נֹהֵ֣ג בַּֽחָכְמָ֑ה וְלֶאֱחֹ֣ז בְּסִכְל֗וּת עַ֣ד אֲשֶׁר־אֶרְאֶ֗ה אֵי־זֶ֨ה ט֜וֹב לִבְנֵ֤י הָאָדָם֙ אֲשֶׁ֤ר יַעֲשׂוּ֙ תַּ֣חַת הַשָּׁמַ֔יִם מִסְפַּ֖ר יְמֵ֥י חַיֵּיהֶֽם׃ ד הִגְדַּ֖לְתִּי מַעֲשָׂ֑י בָּנִ֤יתִי לִי֙ בָּתִּ֔ים נָטַ֥עְתִּי לִ֖י כְּרָמִֽים׃ ה עָשִׂ֣יתִי לִ֔י גַּנּ֖וֹת וּפַרְדֵּסִ֑ים וְנָטַ֥עְתִּי בָהֶ֖ם עֵ֥ץ כָּל־פֶּֽרִי׃ ו עָשִׂ֥יתִי לִ֛י

a. The translation "enjoyment" is opposed to (a) "happiness," which would indicate a greater sense of contentment and a condition, or (b) "joy," which might also be understood to suggest depth of the feeling or its longevity, neither of which is implied by Kohelet's uses of the term. (Note that henceforth, "take joy" implies "enjoyment.")
b. Literally, "see what beneficence is," also implying enjoyment. See 7:14, the only parallel use of *tov*, "good" (i.e., beneficence) with the preposition "*be-*," implying this exceptional meaning. Cf. also Ps. 25:13 and possibly Job 21:13; 36:11.

בְּרֵכוֹת מַיִם לְהַשְׁקוֹת מֵהֶם יַעַר צוֹמֵחַ עֵצִים: ז קָנִיתִי עֲבָדִים וּשְׁפָחוֹת
וּבְנֵי־בַיִת הָיָה לִי גַּם מִקְנֶה בָקָר וָצֹאן הַרְבֵּה הָיָה לִי מִכֹּל שֶׁהָיוּ לְפָנַי
בִּירוּשָׁלָ͏ִם: ח כָּנַסְתִּי לִי גַּם־כֶּסֶף וְזָהָב וּסְגֻלַּת מְלָכִים וְהַמְּדִינוֹת עָשִׂיתִי
לִי שָׁרִים וְשָׁרוֹת וְתַעֲנוּגֹת בְּנֵי הָאָדָם שִׁדָּה וְשִׁדּוֹת: ט וְגָדַלְתִּי וְהוֹסַפְתִּי
מִכֹּל שֶׁהָיָה לְפָנַי בִּירוּשָׁלָ͏ִם אַף חָכְמָתִי עָמְדָה לִּי: י וְכֹל אֲשֶׁר שָׁאֲלוּ
עֵינַי לֹא אָצַלְתִּי מֵהֶם לֹא־מָנַעְתִּי אֶת־לִבִּי מִכָּל־שִׂמְחָה כִּי־לִבִּי שָׂמֵחַ
מִכָּל־עֲמָלִי וְזֶה־הָיָה חֶלְקִי מִכָּל־עֲמָלִי: יא וּפָנִיתִי אֲנִי בְּכָל־מַעֲשַׂי
שֶׁעָשׂוּ יָדַי וּבֶעָמָל שֶׁעָמַלְתִּי לַעֲשׂוֹת וְהִנֵּה הַכֹּל הֶבֶל וּרְעוּת רוּחַ וְאֵין
יִתְרוֹן תַּחַת הַשָּׁמֶשׁ:

2:3 I probed with my heart, to tempt my flesh with wine (my heart still conducting itself with wisdom) and to grab hold of folly, until I might see which is best for mankind to do under the heavens in their few days of life. **4** I undertook great projects.[a] I built myself houses and I planted myself vineyards. **5** I made myself gardens and groves, and I planted therein every kind of fruit tree. **6** I made myself pools of water, to irrigate thereby a forest of flourishing trees. **7** I bought male and female slaves, and I [even] had second-generation slaves[b] for myself. I also had for myself more cattle, both herds and flocks, than all who preceded me in Jerusalem. **8** I further amassed for myself silver and gold and treasure of kings and provinces; and I got myself male and female singers, as well as mankind's luxuries – coffers[9] and coffers of them. **9** So I increased and accumulated more than anyone before me in Jerusalem, as my wisdom still stood by me. **10** I withheld from my eyes nothing they sought, and denied my heart no enjoyment; rather, my heart enjoyed the fruit of my toil. Such was my portion from the fruit of my toil. **11** Then I, I focused on all my achievements my hands had achieved, and on the spoils that I had toiled to achieve – and behold, all this is vapor and anguish, and there is no advantage under the sun.

a. Alternatively, "I increased my assets."
b. That is, children of purchased slaves, implying ongoing wealth; literally, "children of the house."

This description arouses one's suspicions. As told, the tale is one of an "experiment," designed as such from the start. But when did the experimenter begin to sense the failure of wealth to satisfy? As told, the evaluation came only at the end (v. 11). However, the "then" of verse 11 leads to a suspicion that the recollection of all this as an "experiment" suffers from retrospective reframing.

The resounding repetitions of "for myself" throughout the paragraph focus the reader's attention on the speaker's exclusive self-concern. In this tale, there is no royal "experiment" of helping the king's citizens, whether in general or specifically the downtrodden.

This third category of the experiment (wealth) has a tantalizing relation to the second, enjoyment, which he did achieve through wealth (v. 10). As before (v. 2:2), enjoyment is not the answer sought, although the dismissal is somewhat veiled. (In 2:2, laughter is dismissed declaratively, but enjoyment only in a rhetorical question; in verse 2:11, wealth is dismissed, but not necessarily enjoyment). This will be of import later, as Kohelet often returns to enjoyment as a "default" recommendation (i.e., the best one can get, since nothing else seems to be available).

Verse 10 may be in direct contrast to Numbers 15:39, a warning against pursuing false pleasures: "that you not follow your heart and eyes." (Solomon, the model for Kohelet, was considered a sinner in later life – 1 Kings 11:1–13.)

FOURTH EXPERIMENT: WISE MAN AND FOOL

בּ:יב וּפָנִיתִי אֲנִי לִרְאוֹת חָכְמָה וְהוֹלֵלוֹת וְסִכְלוּת כִּי ׀ מֶה הָאָדָם שֶׁיָּבוֹא
אַחֲרֵי הַמֶּלֶךְ אֵת אֲשֶׁר־כְּבָר עָשׂוּהוּ: יג וְרָאִיתִי אָנִי שֶׁיֵּשׁ יִתְרוֹן לַחָכְמָה
מִן־הַסִּכְלוּת כִּיתְרוֹן הָאוֹר מִן־הַחֹשֶׁךְ: יד הֶחָכָם עֵינָיו בְּרֹאשׁוֹ וְהַכְּסִיל
בַּחֹשֶׁךְ הוֹלֵךְ וְיָדַעְתִּי גַם־אָנִי שֶׁמִּקְרֶה אֶחָד יִקְרֶה אֶת־כֻּלָּם: טו וְאָמַרְתִּי
אֲנִי בְּלִבִּי כְּמִקְרֵה הַכְּסִיל גַּם־אֲנִי יִקְרֵנִי וְלָמָּה חָכַמְתִּי אֲנִי אָז יֹתֵר
וְדִבַּרְתִּי בְלִבִּי שֶׁגַּם־זֶה הָבֶל: טז כִּי אֵין זִכְרוֹן לֶחָכָם עִם־הַכְּסִיל לְעוֹלָם
בְּשֶׁכְּבָר הַיָּמִים הַבָּאִים הַכֹּל נִשְׁכָּח וְאֵיךְ יָמוּת הֶחָכָם עִם־הַכְּסִיל:
יז וְשָׂנֵאתִי אֶת־הַחַיִּים כִּי רַע עָלַי הַמַּעֲשֶׂה שֶׁנַּעֲשָׂה תַּחַת הַשֶּׁמֶשׁ כִּי־
הַכֹּל הֶבֶל וּרְעוּת רוּחַ:

2:12 Thus I, I focused on observing wisdom and depravity and folly[a] –
indeed, what will this man who succeeds the king be like, with all these
achievements?[b] **13** So I, I saw that there is an advantage to wisdom over
folly, like the advantage of light over darkness:

> **14** the wise man has his eyes in his head,
> whereas a dolt walks in darkness.

Yet I know, I do, that a single destiny[c] is destined for all. **15** So I, I
said in my heart: "The destiny of the dolt is also destined for me; for
what advantage, then, have I become wise?" And I spoke in my heart,
that this too is vapor, **16** because neither the wise man nor the dolt is
remembered forever; for everything is forgotten when the days to come
have already arrived[10] – how the wise man dies just like the dolt! **17** So I
hated life, for I was appalled[d] at all the accomplishments accomplished
under the sun, for everything is vapor and anguish.

This section, like others to come, juxtaposes contradictory life evidence: a
sensed advantage (and verse 14 may have been a known aphorism) outweighed
by the understanding that there would be no differential repercussions. These
biographical sections continue to afford a glimpse into Kohelet's feelings
("hated life, for I was appalled," v. 17, an extreme expression of bitterness).

FIFTH EXPERIMENT: HEIRS AND TOIL

בּ:יח וְשָׂנֵאתִי אֲנִי אֶת־כָּל־עֲמָלִי שֶׁאֲנִי עָמֵל תַּחַת הַשָּׁמֶשׁ שֶׁאַנִּיחֶנּוּ
לָאָדָם שֶׁיִּהְיֶה אַחֲרָי: יט וּמִי יוֹדֵעַ הֶחָכָם יִהְיֶה אוֹ סָכָל וְיִשְׁלַט בְּכָל־
עֲמָלִי שֶׁעָמַלְתִּי וְשֶׁחָכַמְתִּי תַּחַת הַשָּׁמֶשׁ גַּם־זֶה הָבֶל: כ וְסַבּוֹתִי אֲנִי

a. "Depravity and folly" is possibly a hendiadys, two terms indicating a single phenomenon.
In any case, their role here is more or less as a control group, as Kohelet tests wisdom even
by its alternatives.
b. Verse 12 is uncertain in details. The sense seems to be a contemplation of the value of
wisdom, motivated by the thought that his successor will not have the means to carry out
this "test." He later returns (v. 18ff.) to the subject of his successor.
c. "Single destiny" means either the fact of being forgotten, as immediately emphasized,
or death, as this term implies in 3:19 and 9:2–3. Some interpreters translate this term as
"rule of chance," as it is used in Ruth 2:3 and in 1 Sam. 6:9; 20:26. In any case, destiny does
not imply preordination so much as a bad turn.
d. "Appalled." From the root translated elsewhere as "evil," "bad," "calamitous," or "detriment."

לִיַאֵשׁ אֶת־לִבִּי עַל כָּל־הֶעָמָל שֶׁעָמַלְתִּי תַּחַת הַשָּׁמֶשׁ: כֹּא כִּי־יֵשׁ אָדָם
שֶׁעֲמָלוֹ בְּחָכְמָה וּבְדַעַת וּבְכִשְׁרוֹן וּלְאָדָם שֶׁלֹּא עָמַל־בּוֹ יִתְּנֶנּוּ חֶלְקוֹ
גַּם־זֶה הֶבֶל וְרָעָה רַבָּה: כֹּב כִּי מֶה־הֹוֶה לָאָדָם בְּכָל־עֲמָלוֹ וּבְרַעְיוֹן
לִבּוֹ שֶׁהוּא עָמֵל תַּחַת הַשָּׁמֶשׁ: כֹּג כִּי כָל־יָמָיו מַכְאֹבִים וָכַעַס עִנְיָנוֹ
גַּם־בַּלַּיְלָה לֹא־שָׁכַב לִבּוֹ גַּם־זֶה הֶבֶל הוּא:

2:18 So, too, I hated all the spoils for which I had toiled under the sun, for I shall leave it to the man who will succeed me, **19** and who knows whether he will be a wise man or a fool? Yet he will have authority over all my spoils for which I toiled so wisely under the sun. This too is vapor. **20** And so I turned my heart toward despair regarding all the spoils for which I had toiled under the sun. **21** For sometimes a man, the fruit of whose toil was gained through wisdom, knowledge, and skill, leaves it as a portion to someone who did not toil for it. This, too, is vapor, a great evil. **22** For what does a man get for all his toil and his heart's anxiety[11] in his toil[a] under the sun? **23** Indeed through all his days, pains and vexation are his concern, and even at night his heart does not lie still. This, too, is truly vapor.

Combining the foci of verses 1–11 (wealth) and 12–17 (wise man and fool), Kohelet moves on to despairing of the heir(s) to his fortune. The text also affords further glimpses into his emotional reactions: "hate" (picked up from a previous verse), "despair" at the end, and, looking back, "anxiety," "pains," and "vexation" while accumulating wealth.

The absence of any hint of progeny here (one would probably not relate to the one succeeding him in so cold a manner were the successor his son) and elsewhere lead many to believe that Kohelet had no children, augmenting the sense of loneliness.[b] (This is yet another indication that while this "king" is based on Solomon, he is independent of him. Solomon had many children.) Note the insertion here of a text in the third person (vv. 21–23), as if Kohelet were observing others, which at first seems an effective literary reflection of his own pain. However, it also serves as a foreshadowing of part II, where he observes others.

a. This use of the word "toil" is very close to the original meaning of the term, emphasizing suffering.
b. See the commentary on 7:26–29 and Review Essays 1.2.

FROM BIOGRAPHY TOWARD ADVICE, AND BACK TO OVERVIEW

בּ:כד אֵין־טוֹב בָּאָדָם שֶׁיֹּאכַל וְשָׁתָה וְהֶרְאָה אֶת־נַפְשׁוֹ טוֹב בַּעֲמָלוֹ
גַּם־זֹה רָאִיתִי אָנִי כִּי מִיַּד הָאֱלֹהִים הִיא: כה כִּי מִי יֹאכַל וּמִי יָחוּשׁ חוּץ
מִמֶּנִּי: כו כִּי לְאָדָם שֶׁטוֹב לְפָנָיו נָתַן חָכְמָה וְדַעַת וְשִׂמְחָה וְלַחוֹטֶא נָתַן
עִנְיָן לֶאֱסוֹף וְלִכְנוֹס לָתֵת לְטוֹב לִפְנֵי הָאֱלֹהִים גַּם־זֶה הֶבֶל וּרְעוּת רוּחַ:

2:24 There is nothing better for a man than to consume and drink
and let his appetite see benefit by way of the fruit of his toil: for this, I
have seen, comes from the hand of God. **25** For who should eat or take
pleasure[a] if not I?[b] **26** Indeed He has given wisdom and knowledge and
enjoyment to the man who is good in His presence,[c] but to the failure
He has given a concern to amass and hoard – [only] to give [it all] to
the one who is good in God's presence. This, too, is vapor and anguish.

This concluding paragraph is appropriately dominated by the term *tov*, here
"better," "benefit," and "good" (twice).

Just as one finally feels that Kohelet is moving toward offering advice (vv.
24–26a–b), it turns out that the possibility of acting on his advice – to enjoy
as best one can – is not inherently in one's control, but is only an occasional
opportunity that seems assigned by God for unfathomable reasons. The irony
is that the opportunity to enjoy is given to one who is good in His presence
(i.e., "fortunate enough to merit God's beneficence," a qualifier that will seem
more and more arbitrary as one reads on). Further, if one may label that
person as well as the "failure" according to their fates, ironically *both* reflect
Kohelet's earlier self-descriptions.

a. The translation of the Hebrew word as a feeling ("take pleasure") is based on rabbinic
usage. Some hold that on the basis of rabbinic parallels the word should relate to a *negative*
feeling, approximately, "suffer," which then leads to the alternative translation listed in the
note that follows.
b. Translated here as by Saadia Gaon, verse 25 restates in first person the reservations about
having an unworthy heir. Sforno took it as advice to use up one's wealth, leaving nothing
for any heir. Alternatively, it could be emended (Hebrew, *mi-menu* for *mi-meni*, according
to most interpreters, based on some ancient versions and manuscripts), "for who can
eat or suffer [see previous note] if not owing to Him?" This would be a reinforcement of
verse 24 which fits the continuing use of third-person pronouns for God also in verse 26.
c. This and subsequent uses of this phrase indicate the fact of receiving beneficence from
God, not necessarily virtue. (See Review Essays 4. 2, on the term "good.")

This final paragraph of the section confronts God's role. In chapter 1, the mega-phenomena of nature were seen as trapped in endless repetition. Moreover, since the beginning of chapter 2, man has been an assertive and active searcher, certainly engendering change in his own situation. God appears here as the ultimate true actor, but one who, from man's point of view, is arbitrary.

The pseudo-autobiography ends with "vapor," echoing several previous references (2:1, 11, 17, 23, 26), including the opening overview of the book (1:2).

Part I, Section 3

The Song of Times and Seasons (3:1–15)

ג א לַכֹּל זְמָן וְעֵת לְכָל־חֵפֶץ תַּחַת הַשָּׁמָיִם: ב עֵת לָלֶדֶת וְעֵת לָמוּת
עֵת לָטַעַת וְעֵת לַעֲקוֹר נָטוּעַ: ג עֵת לַהֲרוֹג וְעֵת לִרְפּוֹא עֵת לִפְרוֹץ
וְעֵת לִבְנוֹת: ד עֵת לִבְכּוֹת וְעֵת לִשְׂחוֹק עֵת סְפוֹד וְעֵת רְקוֹד: ה עֵת
לְהַשְׁלִיךְ אֲבָנִים וְעֵת כְּנוֹס אֲבָנִים עֵת לַחֲבוֹק וְעֵת לִרְחֹק מֵחַבֵּק:
ו עֵת לְבַקֵּשׁ וְעֵת לְאַבֵּד עֵת לִשְׁמוֹר וְעֵת לְהַשְׁלִיךְ: ז עֵת לִקְרוֹעַ וְעֵת
לִתְפּוֹר עֵת לַחֲשׁוֹת וְעֵת לְדַבֵּר: ח עֵת לֶאֱהֹב וְעֵת לִשְׂנֹא עֵת מִלְחָמָה
וְעֵת שָׁלוֹם:

3 **1** For everything there is a season, and a time for every
pursuit[a] under the heavens:

2 a time to bear,[b] and a time to die;

a time to plant and a time to uproot the planted;

3 a time to kill and a time to heal;

a time to break through and a time to build;

4 a time to weep and a time to laugh;

a time for[c] wailing and a time for dancing;

---

a. "Pursuit" here (and in vv. 3:17; 5:7 [see note there]; 8:6) is from the root *ch-f-ts*, elsewhere
in Ecclesiastes meaning "desire." When applied to "death" (v. 2) it would imply the more
neutral "development" or "acceptance."

b. Some translators prefer "to be born," based not on the verb form, but on parallelism.
However, all the other verbs in the poem are either a matter of optimal choice or of acceptance of a fate, neither of which fits "to be born."

c. In verses 4, 5, and 8, "for" (prescriptive) might be "of" (descriptive). "For" has been chosen because of the parallelism in verse 5. Verse 1 might also be prescriptive or descriptive.

5 a time to discard stones and a time for gathering stones;[a]
a time to embrace and a time to forgo embracing;
6 a time to seek and a time to lose;
a time to keep and a time to discard;
7 a time to reap and a time to sow;
a time to be silent and a time to speak;
8 a time to love and a time to hate;
a time for war and a time for peace.

Kohelet closes the first unit with a poem whose balanced composition reflects its content. The opening poem dealt with the physical universe, whereas the perspective in this one is an observation of society, and in that way segues into part II, an extended unit of cycles of observation of and advice to others.

Shifting between description and prescription, the poem glides between two extremes of interpretation: determinism (all is in God's hands and there is no human choice) and advice (when to act), while never quite reaching either. As determinism, it would contradict not only many biblical passages, but also the very assumptions that underlie Kohelet's subsequent sections of advice and instruction. As advice, its effectiveness is dependent on fathoming what the specific times are and then making plans in light of the "rhythm" of life. However, one cannot know when the times are coming, and parts of the poem are much too deterministic (particularly death) to allow for this interpretation. Elsewhere, Kohelet clarifies that these times cannot be known (e.g., 8:17).

The poem floats, then, on a sense of order beyond control, a sense of balance that may not be obvious at any one moment, and a sense that one might (though not through steps in his control) find his actions coordinated with cosmically proper times. Negatives and positives appear in changing order, possibly reflecting a lack of regularity or overall pattern. The meta-message is a world filled with opposites (each pair is mutually exclusive at any one moment; they differ in that some are complementary, some conflicting, and some compensatory), and, out of context, the poem could be read as

a. The phrase is unclear, variously interpreted as related to construction, agriculture, or (as a metaphor) sexual activity. The paucity of metaphor throughout the poem (and particularly in its first half) argues for a direct interpretation, but the four-phrase division by verses, *if* the four items are related, would argue for the sexual implication. That said, there is no biblical or other early basis for this metaphor, just a later rabbinic midrashic suggestion.

ultimately reassuring or ultimately frustrating. The details vary in the degree of control that a man might have by either being aware of or acting upon the knowledge of the larger picture, and every detail is balanced by the (sobering or comforting) indication that the opposing notion also has its time.

The poem includes fourteen paired points or, according to the verse division, seven verses of four points each. In the Bible, seven often indicates a complete number and four occasionally does so as well (e.g., the four directions and the four kingdoms in Daniel 8:22), both suggesting comprehensiveness. Moreover, most of the couplets can be seen as examples of rhetorical merism, two extremes meant to indicate an entirety. As in the opening poem of part I (vv. 1:4–7), which might include the four basic elements, the useless struggle to gain advantage is set against an overwhelmingly formidable pattern of stagnation at the highest level, engulfing all apparent change as ultimately ephemeral. The pairings and groupings of four are provocative, and readers are properly drawn to explore them as poetry. No pattern emerges as definitive.

The poem as an independent entity bears constant reconfrontation in its multivalence. In the next verses, however, it is given a focused interpretation, toward the side of frustration. (As in the case of the opening poem, one cannot know, within the book's conceit that Kohelet is a living author, whether it is implied that this was once a separate piece that he wrote and then reused or whether the final framework was originally inherent to the poem's composition[12]). As in the case of the first poem, if there was a refocusing, the text alerts the reader to the possibility of change in Kohelet's affect and positions.

THE POEM'S IMPLICATION AND A FIRST RESORT TO ENJOYMENT

ג:ט מַה־יִּתְרוֹן הָעוֹשֶׂה בַּאֲשֶׁר הוּא עָמֵל:

3:9 What advantage does one achieve through his toil?

Kohelet proceeds to his application of the forgoing poem, brutally at first (v. 9, which can range from "Man cannot affect anything" to "Given a pattern I cannot fathom, what good is it to act?"), limiting its inherent multivalence, as was done to the opening poem. Now the regular time pattern is more focused, not as a prescription of how to act or as a reassuring balance in the universe, but as a careful divine design that man cannot comprehend. Verse 9 echoes 1:3 ("What advantage can man gain through all the spoils for which he toils under the sun?"), hermetically enclosing the opening of Kohelet's words in a grand chiasmus (no advantage – poem about the world – his biographical experiment – poem about the world – no advantage). After appending a recommendation to appreciate enjoyment when one finds it (as he ended his biographical account), Kohelet proceeds in the next unit to observe the world and offer advice as to how to live best in a world that does not seem to reward one's efforts.

גֶּי רָאִיתִי אֶת־הָעִנְיָן אֲשֶׁר נָתַן אֱלֹהִים לִבְנֵי הָאָדָם לַעֲנוֹת בּוֹ: יא אֶת־
הַכֹּל עָשָׂה יָפֶה בְעִתּוֹ גַּם אֶת־הָעֹלָם נָתַן בְּלִבָּם מִבְּלִי אֲשֶׁר לֹא־יִמְצָא
הָאָדָם אֶת־הַמַּעֲשֶׂה אֲשֶׁר־עָשָׂה הָאֱלֹהִים מֵרֹאשׁ וְעַד־סוֹף: יב יָדַעְתִּי
כִּי אֵין טוֹב בָּם כִּי אִם־לִשְׂמוֹחַ וְלַעֲשׂוֹת טוֹב בְּחַיָּיו: יג וְגַם כָּל־הָאָדָם
שֶׁיֹּאכַל וְשָׁתָה וְרָאָה טוֹב בְּכָל־עֲמָלוֹ מַתַּת אֱלֹהִים הִיא:

3:10 I have seen the concerns that God has given humankind to be concerned[a] with: **11** He has done everything in its appropriate time. He also instilled eternity into their heart,[b] but without man ever finding out the deed(s) God has done, from beginning to end.

12 I know that nothing is better within these[c] than enjoying and acting beneficially[d] in his lifetime; **13** and indeed, any man who consumes and drinks and sees benefit from all the fruit of his toil – it is gift from God.

It is here that Kohelet first clearly proposes his prime antidote to his frustration, a partial solution he will repeat often: find a little enjoyment if and when you can (v. 12). He experimented with and observed enjoyment (2:2, 10, 26) and found it insufficient, but he nevertheless concludes that it is as good as one can get.

גֶּיד יָדַעְתִּי כִּי כָּל־אֲשֶׁר יַעֲשֶׂה הָאֱלֹהִים הוּא יִהְיֶה לְעוֹלָם עָלָיו אֵין

a. A pun, for the term "concerned" could also mean "afflicted." ("I have seen the affliction that God gave … to be afflicted with." The two terms have identical root letters, '-n-h.) The verse recalls and echoes 1:13.
b. That is, the desire to know and understand beyond the reaches of time – a view noted by Ibn Ezra.
c. That is, either the concerns (v. 10) or the deeds (v. 11).
d. Literally "do good," a phrase that in Ecclesiastes indicates doing the right thing at the right time for one's benefit. See Review Essays 4.2.

לְהוֹסִיף וּמִמֶּנּוּ אֵין לִגְרֹעַ וְהָאֱלֹהִים עָשָׂה שֶׁיִּרְאוּ מִלְּפָנָיו: טו מַה־שֶּׁהָיָה
כְּבָר הוּא וַאֲשֶׁר לִהְיוֹת כְּבָר הָיָה וְהָאֱלֹהִים יְבַקֵּשׁ אֶת־נִרְדָּף:

3:14 I know that whatever God does will be for eternity:

> Nothing can[a] be added to it
> and nothing can be taken from it –

and God has acted so that they fear in His presence.

> **15** What is occurring already existed [before],
> And what is to occur already exists,

and God seeks repetition.[b]

Kohelet's advice is set against his restated reading of the poem of the "times" (v. 14), now seen as woven into a pattern of oppressive, unalterable repetition, the "big" picture, which "little" man cannot affect. One can almost feel the inability to escape.

The "fear" in verse 14 recalls a traditional biblical value: fear of God, but it really represents a radical change. "Qohelet calls on his hearers to 'fear God' (5:6; 7:15–18; 8:12–13) but…the contexts of these passages [show] that the fear advocated here is that of fright before a powerful and dangerous being, not respect or awe for a mighty and compassionate deity."[13]

Verses 14 and 15 echo other verses: Verse 14 repeats "eternity" from verse 11, there an object of man's burning curiosity, now a prison from which man cannot escape. The verse as a whole is a daring variation on Deuteronomy 4:2 and 13:1, there a proscription against adding to or subtracting from God's commandments. Thus the traditional demand for scrupulous care with laws (Deuteronomy) is redirected toward man's inability to change what God has done.[c] Verse 15 echoes 1:9 (the poem of nonchanging cycles), binding the opening section of the book with this poem of the seasons, all leading to endless, impenetrable repetition.

Verses 3:10–15 can be seen as an addendum to part I, coming after the framing verse, 3:9 ("What advantage…?"). However, looking ahead these verses also establish a format that will be repeated (with variations) another

a. Alternatively, "may," and so the next usage.
b. Uncertain – literally, "what is chased."
c. However, late Hebrew allows for ambiguity here, because it is also possible to translate verse 14 as "Nothing *may be* (instead of can be) added…," that is, a prohibition.

six times: observation of the world leading to advice, each time prescribing a little happiness. The six sections of part II all begin with "see" and end with "enjoy" (as anticipated by verses 10–12 here). The pattern is actually clear enough in this addendum to part I to justify seeing it as the first of seven sections within part II as well.[a]

The divisions in this commentary reflect the "see … enjoyment" structure. As the text proceeds, it will add more and more detailed advice.

a. I have, however, chosen to include it in part I in light of the connection between 3:15 and 1:9. In addition, these verses do not share the quality of close observation of others that marks part II. This could still be a purposefully bridging double use, this paragraph *both* concluding part I and beginning part II. Verses 11:9–10 also share this quality of bridging, in that case, between parts II and III.

Kohelet's Words Part II

The Choices of Life (3:16–11:8)

Part II, Section 1

Everything Equal, Everything Evil (3:16–22)

ג:טז וְעֹוד רָאִיתִי תַּחַת הַשָּׁמֶשׁ מְקֹום הַמִּשְׁפָּט שָׁמָּה הָרֶשַׁע וּמְקֹום
הַצֶּדֶק שָׁמָּה הָרָשַׁע: יז אָמַרְתִּי אֲנִי בְּלִבִּי אֶת־הַצַּדִּיק וְאֶת־הָרָשָׁע
יִשְׁפֹּט הָאֱלֹהִים כִּי־עֵת לְכָל־חֵפֶץ וְעַל כָּל־הַמַּעֲשֶׂה שָׁם: יח אָמַרְתִּי
אֲנִי בְּלִבִּי עַל־דִּבְרַת בְּנֵי הָאָדָם לְבָרָם הָאֱלֹהִים וְלִרְאֹות שֶׁהֶם־בְּהֵמָה
הֵמָּה לָהֶם: יט כִּי מִקְרֶה בְנֵי־הָאָדָם וּמִקְרֶה הַבְּהֵמָה וּמִקְרֶה אֶחָד לָהֶם
כְּמֹות זֶה כֵּן מֹות זֶה וְרוּחַ אֶחָד לַכֹּל וּמֹותַר הָאָדָם מִן־הַבְּהֵמָה אָיִן
כִּי הַכֹּל הָבֶל: כ הַכֹּל הֹולֵךְ אֶל־מָקֹום אֶחָד הַכֹּל הָיָה מִן־הֶעָפָר וְהַכֹּל
שָׁב אֶל־הֶעָפָר: כא מִי יֹודֵעַ רוּחַ בְּנֵי הָאָדָם הָעֹלָה הִיא לְמָעְלָה וְרוּחַ
הַבְּהֵמָה הַיֹּרֶדֶת הִיא לְמַטָּה לָאָרֶץ:

3:16 And further, I have seen under the sun:

> The place of justice – wickedness is there;
>
> The place of righteousness – wickedness is there.

17 I, I said in my heart: "God will judge both the righteous and the wicked, for He has set a time[a] for every pursuit and every act."

18 I, I said in my heart, "As regards men, God is putting them to the test, seeing that they are really animals.[b] **19** For the destiny of mankind

---

a. Reading *sam*, "He has set," for *sham* by shifting a diacritical mark, as many suggest. Without this change, the verse is unclear, reading, "for there is a time for every choice and every act there," with no antecedent for the second "there."

b. The Hebrew of verse 18b is uncertain, and is possibly garbled, as reflected in the translation. Sforno suggested that God wants man to realize that his physical this-worldly being is

and the destiny of animals – they have the same destiny: as the one dies so the other dies, and everything has the same spirit; and the advantage of man over cattle is nothing." Indeed, everything is vapor. **20** Everything goes to the same place; everything was from the dust and everything returns to the dust. **21** Who knows if a man's spirit rises up while an animal's spirit sinks down to the earth?

In verses 3:16–17, we first sense Kohelet's empathy for others. This grows and reappears throughout part II. In this section, he confronts two basic biblical claims: the primacy of justice and the centrality of humankind. Neither is verified by experience. In the first case, reality overwhelms the ideal – perhaps there *should be* justice (evidently, in light of the reaction in verse 17, the reference in verse 16 is to courts), but one does not find it. In verse 17, Kohelet seemingly dilutes his unhappy observation (v. 16) with a small serving of comfort, a belief in some future justice, based on the "balance" implied in the poem of 3:1–8. However, he quickly goes on to deny any assured hope of a future life.

In terms of the second claim, the apparent identical fate of man and animal (v. 20), the text is written in light of the Creation story in Genesis.ᵃ There, soon after man is told he will rule over all living creatures, he is informed that he comes from dust and returns to dust.ᵇ In Genesis this indicates an end to man's immortality, not an equivalency to animals. Kohelet interprets "dust to dust," with great irony, as a return to broad "equality" with the other creatures, implying that any other differentiation is speculation. (The idea of a spirit belonging to God, as possibly reflected in Psalm 104:29–30, is evidently ignored as empirically not provable. In any case, Kohelet is *denying* the certainty of any meaningful postlife existence.[14])

The "test" of verse 18 is simply unclear (as is much of the verse), and one should not draw any firm conclusions based thereon.

With the opening critique of the justice system, the "mask" of kingship from the pseudo-autobiography of chapters 1 and 2 starts to fall away. In

---

essentially beastlike. The last four words each include two letters (*h-m*) in the same order, a result of, or the cause of, the confusion. Alternatively, the verse may cite a common lyrical phrase of known meaning then, a meaning now lost to us.
a. See other references, commentary on part I, section 1.
b. Genesis 2:7; 3:19.

antiquity it was the king's role to maintain justice in the land! That mask will continue to fall away, as implied by the text (Kohelet functions as an intimate observer of society) and as reflected in certain details (from his personal knowledge of hard labor to his observations of kingship from a distance).

THE ONLY OPTION: ENJOYMENT

ג:כב וְרָאִיתִי כִּי אֵין טוֹב מֵאֲשֶׁר יִשְׂמַח הָאָדָם בְּמַעֲשָׂיו כִּי־הוּא חֶלְקוֹ
כִּי מִי יְבִיאֶנּוּ לִרְאוֹת בְּמֶה שֶׁיִּהְיֶה אַחֲרָיו:

3:22 So I saw that there is nothing better than that a man enjoy his achievements, since that is his portion. For who can bring him to see what will be after him?

Kohelet again proceeds from what he "sees" to recommend enjoyment, by default, this time in light of the lack of justice and the lack of a superiority of humankind, but also in light of the unknown future.

The core term of part II, section 1 is "everything," possibly reflecting both the equality of men and beasts and the mis-justice applied to wicked and to righteous alike.

Part II, Section 2

Society as Failure (4:1–5:19)

SOCIETAL ILLS

דּ א וְשַׁבְתִּי אֲנִי וָאֶרְאֶה אֶת־כָּל־הָעֲשֻׁקִים אֲשֶׁר נַעֲשִׂים תַּחַת
הַשָּׁמֶשׁ וְהִנֵּה ׀ דִּמְעַת הָעֲשֻׁקִים וְאֵין לָהֶם מְנַחֵם וּמִיַּד עֹשְׁקֵיהֶם
כֹּחַ וְאֵין לָהֶם מְנַחֵם: ב וְשַׁבֵּחַ אֲנִי אֶת־הַמֵּתִים שֶׁכְּבָר מֵתוּ מִן־הַחַיִּים
אֲשֶׁר הֵמָּה חַיִּים עֲדֶנָה: ג וְטוֹב מִשְּׁנֵיהֶם אֵת אֲשֶׁר־עֲדֶן לֹא הָיָה אֲשֶׁר
לֹא־רָאָה אֶת־הַמַּעֲשֶׂה הָרָע אֲשֶׁר נַעֲשָׂה תַּחַת הַשָּׁמֶשׁ:

4 ¹ And I, I saw once again all the oppressions done under the sun: for here are the tears of the oppressed,[a] but they have no comforter; and power is in the hands of their oppressors – but they have no comforter.[b] 2 Thus I commend the dead, those already dead, more than the living, still living; 3 but better off than both of them is one who has yet to exist, who has not seen the evil deed done under the sun.

Kohelet opens a longer section of observations, socially based. His initial foray into the public sphere in the last section turns now into a full-blown arena of observation. Having bemoaned injustice in the last section, he now feels overwhelmed by the fact that individuals neither help nor comfort the oppressed (the "evil deed" in verse 3 may apply to either or both). One should recall that Kohelet's purpose here is to observe the world, not improve it. It is going beyond the book's scope to conclude that he would or did ignore the unfortunate, not seeking opportunities to improve their lot.

His conclusions are extreme in verses 2 and 3. One can again feel Kohelet's

a. This is the same Hebrew word as "oppressions," used earlier in the verse.
b. This phrase is possibly borrowed from Lamentations 1:2, there indicating no comforter for destroyed Jerusalem. Its repeated use in this verse implies repeated occurrences, all without a comforter (Ibn Ezra).

pain, even though he does not suffer the oppression but only observes it. Thus there is a double emphasis on suffering, both the oppression itself and the witnessing of it. The reader is granted a touching glimpse of Kohelet and the misery he feels in his observation.

Here Kohelet opens with a repetition, "but they have no comforter," recalling the repetition that opened the previous section ("wickedness is there," 3:16), literarily tying the two sections, which are in any case similar.

ד:ד וְרָאִיתִי אֲנִי אֶת־כָּל־עָמָל וְאֵת כָּל־כִּשְׁרוֹן הַמַּעֲשֶׂה כִּי הִיא קִנְאַת־
אִישׁ מֵרֵעֵהוּ גַּם־זֶה הֶבֶל וּרְעוּת רוּחַ: ה הַכְּסִיל חֹבֵק אֶת־יָדָיו וְאֹכֵל
אֶת־בְּשָׂרוֹ: ו טוֹב מְלֹא כַף נָחַת מִמְּלֹא חָפְנַיִם עָמָל וּרְעוּת רוּחַ:

4:4 And I, I saw that all toil and skillful conduct are essentially one man's envy of his fellowman. This too is vapor and anguish!

> 5 The fool folds his hands
> and so consumes his flesh.
> 6 Better is a handful[a] of tranquility
> than two fistfuls of the fruit of toil and anguish.

Turning then to labor and toil, and having reduced them to jealousy of neighbors, Kohelet first bemoans the frustration ("vapor" and "anguish"), and then cites two opposite extremes of the wrong reactions to this truth – the fool, who does nothing and starves,[b] and one who puts in too much effort.[15]

ז וְשַׁבְתִּי אֲנִי וָאֶרְאֶה הֶבֶל תַּחַת הַשָּׁמֶשׁ: ח יֵשׁ אֶחָד וְאֵין שֵׁנִי גַּם בֵּן וָאָח
אֵין־לוֹ וְאֵין קֵץ לְכָל־עֲמָלוֹ גַּם־עֵינָיו [עֵינוֹ] לֹא־תִשְׂבַּע עֹשֶׁר וּלְמִי | אֲנִי
עָמֵל וּמְחַסֵּר אֶת־נַפְשִׁי מִטּוֹבָה גַּם־זֶה הֶבֶל וְעִנְיַן רָע הוּא: ט טוֹבִים
הַשְּׁנַיִם מִן־הָאֶחָד אֲשֶׁר יֵשׁ־לָהֶם שָׂכָר טוֹב בַּעֲמָלָם: י כִּי אִם־יִפֹּלוּ
הָאֶחָד יָקִים אֶת־חֲבֵרוֹ וְאִילוֹ הָאֶחָד שֶׁיִּפּוֹל וְאֵין שֵׁנִי לַהֲקִימוֹ: יא גַּם
אִם־יִשְׁכְּבוּ שְׁנַיִם וְחַם לָהֶם וּלְאֶחָד אֵיךְ יֵחָם: יב וְאִם־יִתְקְפוֹ הָאֶחָד
הַשְּׁנַיִם יַעַמְדוּ נֶגְדּוֹ וְהַחוּט הַמְשֻׁלָּשׁ לֹא בִמְהֵרָה יִנָּתֵק:

4:7 And I, I saw once again vapor under the sun: 8 when there is one without a companion, even without son or brother; yet there is no end to his toil, his eyes are never sated with riches – "So for whom

---

a. "Handful" probably indicates a small amount (so Seow).

b. For similar sentiment and wording, see the adage cited in Proverbs 6:10; 24:33.

do I toil, while depriving my appetites of benefit?" – this, too is vapor, and an evil matter it is.

9 Two are better than one, for they have good recompense through their toil – 10 for if they fall, the one lifts his comrade, but woe to the one who falls without a second person to raise him. 11 Further, when two lie together they are warm; but how can one get warm? 12 Also, if somebody attacks one, two can stand up to him – and a three-ply cord is not quickly snapped.

The concentration on toil in the previous verses leads to a third societal observation, and a bit of an ironic one at that, for now Kohelet realizes (as have sensitive observers of many eras) that many people are ultimately alone. This observation proceeds smoothly from verse 6.

The touching first-person quotation of verse 8 is possibly the cry of the one who toils (so Rashbam), but it might also be read as an outburst, lending an autobiographical tinge to Kohelet's observation.[16] The verse certainly reflects a personality that is diametrically opposed to the fool of verse 5.

Verses 9–12 expand on the loneliness noted in verses 7–8 by picturing the obverse side of the coin. Even minimal needs become beyond the grasp of the lonely individual, as society often marches on, indifferent to his or her isolation.

ד:יג טוֹב יֶ֫לֶד מִסְכֵּן וְחָכָם מִמֶּ֫לֶךְ זָקֵן וּכְסִיל אֲשֶׁר לֹא־יָדַע לְהִזָּהֵר עוֹד: יד כִּי־מִבֵּית הָסוּרִים יָצָא לִמְלֹךְ כִּי גַּם בְּמַלְכוּתוֹ נוֹלַד רָשׁ: טו רָאִ֫יתִי אֶת־כָּל־הַחַיִּים הַמְהַלְּכִים תַּחַת הַשָּׁמֶשׁ עִם הַיֶּלֶד הַשֵּׁנִי אֲשֶׁר יַעֲמֹד תַּחְתָּיו: טז אֵין־קֵץ לְכָל־הָעָם לְכֹל אֲשֶׁר־הָיָה לִפְנֵיהֶם גַּם הָאַחֲרוֹנִים לֹא יִשְׂמְחוּ־בוֹ כִּי־גַם־זֶה הֶבֶל וְרַעְיוֹן רוּחַ:

4:13 Better a wise poor lad than a foolish old king who no longer knows how to heed admonishment,[a] 14 though he emerged from a dungeon to become king; for during his kingship, too, a pauper is born.[b] 15 I saw all the living walking about under the sun with that lad (the second one) who would stand in his place. 16 There is no end to the people, all

a. Alternatively, "take lessons (from the past)."
b. Verse 14 is subject to many interpretations. All could refer to the youth (the end would read, "even though he was born a pauper during the [previous] kingship" or the whole verse might refer to the king of verse 13, "though he himself rose from a dungeon," etc. However, the general sense of rise and fall is shared by most interpretations.

who went before them; but later ones will take no joy in him.[a] Indeed, this too is vapor and anguish.

Even reaching the pinnacle of the societal heap is not any assurance. Today's king is replaced by tomorrow's upstart, and no memory remains. Though the text is difficult (see the notes), the thrust is clear – (at least) one king is succeeded by an upstart on the rise as there is no permanency to power, but even the second king will ultimately not be appreciated. In verse 16, endless followers have no more import than the endless work above (v. 8). The multiple possible interpretations here may imply that one detail or another is not of the essence – the points remain valid across a range of illustrative stories.

שְׁמֹר רַגְלֶיךָ [רַגְלְךָ] כַּאֲשֶׁר תֵּלֵךְ אֶל־בֵּית הָאֱלֹהִים וְקָרוֹב לִשְׁמֹעַ דּ:יז
מִתֵּת הַכְּסִילִים זָבַח כִּי־אֵינָם יוֹדְעִים לַעֲשׂוֹת רָע:

ה א אַל־תְּבַהֵל עַל־פִּיךָ וְלִבְּךָ אַל־יְמַהֵר לְהוֹצִיא דָבָר לִפְנֵי הָאֱלֹהִים
כִּי הָאֱלֹהִים בַּשָּׁמַיִם וְאַתָּה עַל־הָאָרֶץ עַל־כֵּן יִהְיוּ דְבָרֶיךָ מְעַטִּים:
ב כִּי בָּא הַחֲלוֹם בְּרֹב עִנְיָן וְקוֹל כְּסִיל בְּרֹב דְּבָרִים: ג כַּאֲשֶׁר תִּדֹּר נֶדֶר
לֵאלֹהִים אַל־תְּאַחֵר לְשַׁלְּמוֹ כִּי אֵין חֵפֶץ בַּכְּסִילִים אֵת אֲשֶׁר־תִּדֹּר
שַׁלֵּם: ד טוֹב אֲשֶׁר לֹא־תִדֹּר מִשֶּׁתִּדּוֹר וְלֹא תְשַׁלֵּם: ה אַל־תִּתֵּן אֶת־
פִּיךָ לַחֲטִיא אֶת־בְּשָׂרֶךָ וְאַל־תֹּאמַר לִפְנֵי הַמַּלְאָךְ כִּי שְׁגָגָה הִיא לָמָּה
יִקְצֹף הָאֱלֹהִים עַל־קוֹלֶךָ וְחִבֵּל אֶת־מַעֲשֵׂה יָדֶיךָ: ו כִּי בְרֹב חֲלֹמוֹת
וַהֲבָלִים וּדְבָרִים הַרְבֵּה כִּי אֶת־הָאֱלֹהִים יְרָא:

4:17 Tread carefully when you go to the House of God: more [desirable[b]] is obedience than fools offering sacrifice, for they know nothing of doing evil.

5 [1] Hasten not with your mouth, and let not your heart be quick to utter a word before God. For God is in the heavens and you are on earth; therefore your words should be few –

2 for dreams come in multiple concerns,
　and the voice of the dolt in multiple words.

---

a. Also a difficult verse, with unclear referents (including masses who followed these two kings, masses who followed previous kings, a large number of earlier kings, and lack of appreciation by subsequent generations or subsequent kings).
b. Uncertain. The sense here is that reflected in most commentaries.

3 When you vow a vow to God, do not delay in fulfilling it, for He is not desirous of dolts; what you vow, fulfill. **4** Better that you not vow than that you vow and not fulfill. **5** Do not let your mouth bring your flesh to failure, and do not plead before the messenger[a] that it was an error – why should God be angered by your voice and destroy your handiwork? **6** Rather, despite the multitude of dreams and vapors, and multitudinous words – indeed, fear God.

In the midst of this second section as he observes the world, Kohelet pauses to insert his first extended segment of advice. From this point on, such segments will provide counterpoints to his observations and will be granted a growing centrality. The two present subjects of advice are somewhat related to this observation-based section in that they are both "societal," the first more loosely so (sacrifice and vows[b] being centered in the Temple); the second, corrupt governance, more so.

SACRIFICE AND VOWS. Verse 17 is difficult. The first part presumably compares obedience to sacrifice (i.e., following disobedience), possibly by flippant fools who find in later sacrifice a full alternative to doing right earlier. The next verse implies that dreams often motivate vows.[c] It is of some interest that the "bottom lines" of this short concentration are conventional enough: obedience, caution, fulfilling obligations, and fear of God (cf. 1 Sam. 15:22 – "obedience is better than sacrifice"). Tradition preferred not vowing, but insisted on scrupulous fulfillment once a vow was made (Deut. 23:22–24). This is the first indication that Kohelet's observations do not necessarily lead him out of the normative framework of his society. In fact, "fear God" (5:6) is a traditional, oft-repeated biblical demand, although it takes on new complexity given Kohelet's view of the difficulty in understanding God's workings.

Three phrases deserve particular attention:

1. "Tread carefully when you go" (4:17) is a clever literary introduction to his emphasis on care in what is ostensibly a positive act – pilgrimage.

a. Uncertain whether "whose" or "Whose" (i.e., God's) messenger. This term is used elsewhere of priests and prophets (Mal. 2:7; 3:1).
b. Cf. Deuteronomy 12:17.
c. Alternatively, verse 2 is a known aphorism, comparing the meaningless details of dreams to the meaningless verbosity of fools (so Ibn Ezra).

2. "God is in the heavens and you are on earth" (5:1) reflects the distance from God that Kohelet sees as he looks for evidence of His workings "under the sun."[a]

3. In 5:4 Kohelet smoothly revises the implication of "better" when used as a comparison between two situations. Previously (4:3, 6, 9, 13) the phrase was an observation on life, unrelated to an individual's choice. Now the phrase becomes direct advice (see also 6:9 and particularly chapter 7), part of the incremental turn to advice as the book progresses.

OTHER PHRASES. "Know nothing of wrongdoing" (4:17) is a much disputed phrase, taken here as synecdoche for lacking any true knowledge of what is good and bad. Verse 5:2 seems to warn against both overreacting to one's interpretation of dreams and speaking too much in terms of vows. (Verse 5:2 may have been a known aphorism, structured originally as a play on the term "multitude," which Kohelet now applies to his specific context.) Verse 5:6 picks up the rejection of "multitude" from 5:2. (The Hebrew in v. 2 of "in multiple" is the same as "through the multitude" in v. 6.)

On "fear God" (v. 16), see the commentary on verse 3:14.

ה:ז אִם־עֹשֶׁק רָשׁ וְגֵזֶל מִשְׁפָּט וָצֶדֶק תִּרְאֶה בַמְּדִינָה אַל־תִּתְמַהּ עַל־הַחֵפֶץ כִּי גָבֹהַּ מֵעַל גָּבֹהַּ שֹׁמֵר וּגְבֹהִים עֲלֵיהֶם: ח וְיִתְרוֹן אֶרֶץ בַּכֹּל הִיא [הוּא] מֶלֶךְ לְשָׂדֶה נֶעֱבָד:

5:7 If you see in the province[b] oppression of the poor and deprivation of justice and right, be not amazed at what happens;[c] for a higher official protects a high official, with highest ones above them, **8** and the advantage of land [ownership] is above everything – [even] a king is subject to the field![17]

a. Here Kohelet differs from other biblical claims only by degree. Other verses show awareness both of God's action on earth (e.g., Deut. 4:29) and his distance (e.g., Ps. 115:2), and clearly Kohelet notes God's acts on earth – he simply can neither understand them nor explain their logic.

b. Seow has noted a fine word play in this verse, the Hebrew "province" built on the root *din*, "judgment," implying that justice is absent where it should be present!

c. "Happens" is the term translated "pursuit" in verses 3:1, 17; 8:6, that is, "that which humans pursue and do."

The translation of verses 7 and 8 is uncertain and much debated. The translation above sees the two verses as linked, and is influenced by a presumption of connection to the coming observation on the futility of wealth ("land" here being viewed as a synecdoche for wealth[18]). Here Kohelet's advice, given in light of widespread administrative corruption, is attitudinal ("be not amazed"), not behavioral, which then leads him back to his ongoing observations.

ה:ט אֹהֵב כֶּ֙סֶף֙ לֹֽא־יִשְׂבַּ֣ע כֶּ֔סֶף וּמִֽי־אֹהֵ֥ב בֶּהָמ֖וֹן לֹ֣א תְבוּאָ֑ה גַּם־זֶ֖ה הֶ֑בֶל: י בִּרְבוֹת֙ הַטּוֹבָ֔ה רַבּ֖וּ אוֹכְלֶ֑יהָ וּמַה־כִּשְׁרוֹן֙ לִבְעָלֶ֔יהָ כִּ֖י אִם־רְאִ֥ית [רְא֥וּת] עֵינָֽיו: יא מְתוּקָה֙ שְׁנַ֣ת הָעֹבֵ֔ד אִם־מְעַ֥ט וְאִם־הַרְבֵּ֖ה יֹאכֵ֑ל וְהַשָּׂבָע֙ לֶעָשִׁ֔יר אֵינֶ֛נּוּ מַנִּ֥יחַֽ ל֖וֹ לִישֽׁוֹן: יב יֵ֣שׁ רָעָ֣ה חוֹלָ֔ה רָאִ֖יתִי תַּ֣חַת הַשָּׁ֑מֶשׁ עֹ֛שֶׁר שָׁמ֥וּר לִבְעָלָ֖יו לְרָעָתֽוֹ: יג וְאָבַ֛ד הָעֹ֥שֶׁר הַה֖וּא בְּעִנְיַ֣ן רָ֑ע וְהוֹלִ֣יד בֵּ֔ן וְאֵ֥ין בְּיָד֖וֹ מְאֽוּמָה: יד כַּאֲשֶׁ֤ר יָצָא֙ מִבֶּ֣טֶן אִמּ֔וֹ עָר֛וֹם יָשׁ֥וּב לָלֶ֖כֶת כְּשֶׁבָּ֑א וּמְא֗וּמָה לֹא־יִשָּׂ֤א בַעֲמָלוֹ֙ שֶׁיֹּלֵ֖ךְ בְּיָדֽוֹ: טו וְגַם־זֹה֙ רָעָ֣ה חוֹלָ֔ה כָּל־עֻמַּ֥ת שֶׁבָּ֖א כֵּ֣ן יֵלֵ֑ךְ וּמַה־יִּתְר֣וֹן ל֔וֹ שֶׁיַּעֲמֹ֖ל לָר֑וּחַ: טז גַּ֧ם כָּל־יָמָ֛יו בַּחֹ֥שֶׁךְ יֹאכֵ֖ל וְכָעַ֥ס הַרְבֵּ֖ה וְחָלְי֥וֹ וָקָֽצֶף:

5:9 A lover of silver never has enough silver;
one loving treasure, no[t enough] income.
This, too, is vapor.

10 As goods increase, so do those who consume them;
of what import, then, is skill for those who have it –
just what his eyes get to see!ᵃ

11 A worker's sleep is sweet, whether he consumes little or
much;
but the rich man's abundanceᵇ does not allow him to sleep.

12 There is a debilitating evil I have seen under the sun: wealth kept
for its owner to his detriment,ᶜ 13 as that wealth was lost in some bad
concern, and he begot a son, having nothing in hand. 14 As he left his

a. That is, something concrete to have in hand, implying real but very temporary gain – see parallel phrase, 6:9.
b. An ironic use of the same root as "enough" silver ("enoughness," as it were), 5:9, as Whybray, NCB, p. 100, notes. The root is translated "sated" elsewhere in this commentary.
c. "Detriment" is the same word (ra'ah) as "evil" in this verse, a play on words.

mother's womb, so he must go back, naked as he came. He can take nothing from the fruit of his toil to go in hand. **15** This, then, is also a debilitating evil: as he came, so must he go, and what advantage had he, toiling for the wind? **16** Besides, all his days he consumes in darkness, and [with] much vexation, and debilitation, and anger.

In these two paragraphs, Kohelet eloquently describes the worthlessness of wealth, in its never-ending creation of avarice and in the vagaries of riches, which often disappear. Verses 9, 10, and 11 list three separate proverbs, together making the cumulative point. The next verses illustrate that point with a story. The fact that the beginning of verse 14 can be applied to either the father or the son as "he who leaves naked" (and commentators waste much ink over which is correct) is an eloquent testimony to the cyclical nature of the problem.

Verse 13 augments previous similar scenarios: in 2:19, the heir is possibly a fool; in 4:8 there is no heir. Here there is an heir who gets nothing.

Verse 16 implies that he works through to dark every day before eating. This paragraph includes all the uses of "debilitate" in Ecclesiastes.[a] It provides sharp contrast to the following advice to seek enjoyment.

THE ONLY OPTION: ENJOYMENT

ה:^{יז} הִנֵּה אֲשֶׁר־רָאִיתִי אָנִי טוֹב אֲשֶׁר־יָפֶה לֶאֱכוֹל־וְלִשְׁתּוֹת וְלִרְאוֹת
טוֹבָה בְּכָל־עֲמָלוֹ ׀ שֶׁיַּעֲמֹל תַּחַת־הַשֶּׁמֶשׁ מִסְפַּר יְמֵי־חַיָּו [חַיָּיו]
אֲשֶׁר־נָתַן־לוֹ הָאֱלֹהִים כִּי־הוּא חֶלְקוֹ: ^{יח} גַּם כָּל־הָאָדָם אֲשֶׁר נָתַן־
לוֹ הָאֱלֹהִים עֹשֶׁר וּנְכָסִים וְהִשְׁלִיטוֹ לֶאֱכֹל מִמֶּנּוּ וְלָשֵׂאת אֶת־חֶלְקוֹ
וְלִשְׂמֹחַ בַּעֲמָלוֹ זֹה מַתַּת אֱלֹהִים הִיא: ^{יט} כִּי לֹא הַרְבֵּה יִזְכֹּר אֶת־יְמֵי
חַיָּיו כִּי הָאֱלֹהִים מַעֲנֶה בְּשִׂמְחַת לִבּוֹ:

5:17 Here then, is what I myself saw: it is to one's benefit, most appropriate, to eat, drink, and see benefit through the spoils of his toil under the sun during the few days of life that God has given him; for that is his portion. **18** Also, any man to whom God gives wealth and property, and empowers[b] him to consume his portion and to

---

a. The appearance of "debilitation" in verse 16 actually has a different root, but one closely related to the first two uses.

b. Root is "authority." The same translation ("empower") is used in 6:2.

enjoy the fruits of his toil – that clearly is a gift from God, **19** for he will not brood[a] much over the days of his life because God keeps him[19] concerned with his heart's enjoyment.

Again Kohelet ends a series of observations (now including advice) with the central contention that the best one that can do is to find a little enjoyment. The striking contention that this distracts man from depressing contemplation is unique. It does not detract from the claim that enjoyment is a gift from God,[20] but it may be seen as undermining any other inherent worth of the "gift."

The three core terms of part II, section 2, are "toil/spoils," "see," and "under the sun," reflecting the strong emphasis on societal observation.

a. The root of the word for brood indicates having a memory.

Part II, Section 3 .

The "Best" You Can Do (6:1–7:14)

א יֵשׁ רָעָה אֲשֶׁר רָאִיתִי תַּחַת הַשָּׁמֶשׁ וְרַבָּה הִיא עַל־הָאָדָם: ב אִישׁ
אֲשֶׁר יִתֶּן־לוֹ הָאֱלֹהִים עֹשֶׁר וּנְכָסִים וְכָבוֹד וְאֵינֶנּוּ חָסֵר לְנַפְשׁוֹ ׀
מִכֹּל אֲשֶׁר־יִתְאַוֶּה וְלֹא־יַשְׁלִיטֶנּוּ הָאֱלֹהִים לֶאֱכֹל מִמֶּנּוּ כִּי אִישׁ נָכְרִי
יֹאכְלֶנּוּ זֶה הֶבֶל וָחֳלִי רָע הוּא: ג אִם־יוֹלִיד אִישׁ מֵאָה וְשָׁנִים רַבּוֹת
יִחְיֶה וְרַב ׀ שֶׁיִּהְיוּ יְמֵי־שָׁנָיו וְנַפְשׁוֹ לֹא־תִשְׂבַּע מִן־הַטּוֹבָה וְגַם־קְבוּרָה
לֹא־הָיְתָה לּוֹ אָמַרְתִּי טוֹב מִמֶּנּוּ הַנָּפֶל: ד כִּי־בַהֶבֶל בָּא וּבַחֹשֶׁךְ יֵלֵךְ
וּבַחֹשֶׁךְ שְׁמוֹ יְכֻסֶּה: ה גַּם־שֶׁמֶשׁ לֹא־רָאָה וְלֹא יָדָע נַחַת לָזֶה מִזֶּה:
ו וְאִלּוּ חָיָה אֶלֶף שָׁנִים פַּעֲמַיִם וְטוֹבָה לֹא רָאָה הֲלֹא אֶל־מָקוֹם אֶחָד
הַכֹּל הוֹלֵךְ:

6 ¹ There is an evil I have seen under the sun, an overwhelming[a]
one for man: **2** a person to whom God gives wealth, property,
and honor, so that he does not want for anything his appetite may
crave, but God does not empower him to consume any of it; instead,
a stranger will consume it. This is vapor, and an evil debilitation it is.
3 Even if a man should beget a hundred and live many years – as many
as the days of his years may be – if his appetite is not sated through
his goods, then I say that even the stillbirth, though it was not even
accorded a burial,²¹ is better off than he: **4** although it comes within
vapor and goes into darkness, and in that darkness its very name is
shrouded, **5** and it has neither even seen nor known the sun – there is

a. "Overwhelming" can indicate "widespread" as well (so Rashi). The term is used again
in 8:6.

greater tranquility for the one [stillbirth] than the other [old man],[a] 6 and even if he lived twice a thousand years, but never got to see [any] benefit. Is not everything going to the same place?

Refocusing from society to the individual, this paragraph plumbs the depths of depression. If Kohelet previously concluded that the dead are better than the living, and the unborn more fortunate than both (vv. 4:2–3), he now goes further, using the stillbirth for comparison! Extreme hyperbole marks the section as a whole, from a hundred children, to a two-thousand year existence, to the preference for the stillborn. The paragraph effectively and chillingly reduces the value of life to immediate satisfaction.

The text thus continues in a greatly strengthened restatement of previous observations, including the complaint that all have one fate (a similar previous contention, in 3:21, was somewhat ambiguous). The negative pressure seems to rise, as it approaches an odd turn to better options, which will appear shortly.

The last sentence in verse 6 may have been meant to be read twice, once completing what preceded and once introducing the upcoming phrase – all of man's toil going to his mouth.

ז כָּל־עֲמַל הָאָדָם לְפִיהוּ וְגַם־הַנֶּפֶשׁ לֹא תִמָּלֵא: ח כִּי מַה־יּוֹתֵר לֶחָכָם
מִן־הַכְּסִיל מַה־לֶּעָנִי יוֹדֵעַ לַהֲלֹךְ נֶגֶד הַחַיִּים: ט טוֹב מַרְאֵה עֵינַיִם
מֵהֲלָךְ־נָפֶשׁ גַּם־זֶה הֶבֶל וּרְעוּת רוּחַ:

6:7 All the fruits of man's toil go to his mouth, yet the appetite is not filled.[b] 8 So what advantage has either the wise man over the dolt, or [what advantage over] the pauper who knows how to face life and go on?[c] 9 Better something for the eyes to see[d] than going after one's appetite. This, too, is vapor and anguish.

a. A pun, for the sentence could read, "never even seen the sun or experienced contentment from this or that [i.e., from anything]." Both meanings are implied.
b. That is, satiated.
c. The second half of the verse is simply unclear, but the possible sense is that all levels of human effort or skill bring no advantage, owing to insatiable human appetite.
d. That is, something concrete to have in hand, even if temporary – see a similar phrase in 5:10, and a parallel phrase in 11:9.

With verse 7 recalling Ecclesiastes's opening poem (1:7 – "All the rivers go to the sea, but the sea is never full"), but now on a personal level, Kohelet continues to focus on the individual. This paragraph is also connected to the previous ones by the frequent use of the term "appetite." In verse 9, on the other hand, he anticipates the "relatively better" observations soon to come (in chapter 7).

וי מַה־שֶּׁהָיָה כְּבָר נִקְרָא שְׁמֹו וְנוֹדָע אֲשֶׁר־הוּא אָדָם וְלֹא־יוּכַל לָדִין עִם שֶׁהַתַּקִּיף [שֶׁתַּקִּיף] מִמֶּנּוּ: יא כִּי יֵשׁ־דְּבָרִים הַרְבֵּה מַרְבִּים הָבֶל מַה־יֹּתֵר לָאָדָם: יב כִּי מִי־יוֹדֵעַ מַה־טוֹב לָאָדָם בַּחַיִּים מִסְפַּר יְמֵי־חַיֵּי הֶבְלוֹ וְיַעֲשֵׂם כַּצֵּל אֲשֶׁר מִי־יַגִּיד לָאָדָם מַה־יִּהְיֶה אַחֲרָיו תַּחַת הַשָּׁמֶשׁ:

6:10 Whatever happens has already been designated, and it is known that he is [but] a man, unable to contend with what is stronger than he. **11** Indeed, there are so many things creating so much vapor – what advantage has a man?[a] **12** Indeed, who can know what is best for a man in life – the few days of his life of vapor, which he spends like a shadow[b] – in that who can tell a man what will be after him under the sun?

Again Kohelet returns to the opening poem (now to 1:9) while bringing the observation of the physical universe there to an individual level here. He splits verse 1:9 ("What was is what will be...and there is nothing new under the sun") between the two halves, substituting the individual man for the earlier combined sun, wind, rivers, and time. Here he also reaches new depths of frustration by echoing "man" of the opening of the two previous paragraphs of this section (6:1, 7), only to show how impotent man is ("unable to contend – so many things creating vapor – who can know – days like a shadow"). As "man" in Hebrew is the same word as "Adam," verse 10 may undermine the Creation story (through a pun), wherein Adam, not God, "designates" (gives names to) the animals (Gen. 2:20).

The echoing of 1:9 creates a hermetic inclusion to the book to this point, all the more effective in that it is a secondary structure and, in terms of the

a. That is, "What advantage can he achieve?"
b. This implies fast-fleeting days, "shadow" referring to the time, not the man. Alternatively, "which he should consider as [no more than a fleeting] shadow" (so Ibn Ezra).

primary structure, it is placed in the middle of part II, the series of sections of observations and advice. However, from this point, there is a slight tip in the balance within the book. Although much will remain unchanged (all is vapor, there is no certainty, there is no observable justice, a little enjoyment remains the option of choice, and so on), there is increasing emphasis on advice as to how to get along. Moreover, the personalization of concern with death (here reflected in "his life of vapor," v. 11) and the immediate advice to gain happiness through personal acquaintance with death in the coming verses (7:1–4) reflect the new emphases of this "second half." (I detail further developments below.)

One literary sign of this slight change is the disappearance of the term "anguish," its last appearance in 6:9 marking the traditional physical middle of the book. A second indication might be the use in verse 11 of "creating so much vapor" (which literally could be read "multiplying vapor"), which can be seen as a subtle midpoint between the two end verses, 1:2 and 12:8, each of which uses "vapor" a number of times.

There is an appropriate sad end to chapter 6 – what is "known" is how weak man is; what is "unknowable" is what to do in life.

The immediate continuation of this section, in 7:1–14, provides some minimal relief by listing goals that are, despite all, better than others.[22] The section ends with this group of verses. To a degree, they replace the usual section-concluding appearance of "enjoy" as the counterweight to observed futility. Nevertheless, the term "take delight" in 7:14 at the end of the section is the linguistic equivalent of "enjoy" (see 2:1, with footnote).

NEVERTHELESS, THERE ARE BETTER CHOICES

א טוֹב שֵׁם מִשֶּׁמֶן טוֹב וְיוֹם הַמָּוֶת מִיּוֹם הִוָּלְדוֹ: ב טוֹב לָלֶכֶת אֶל־
בֵּית־אֵבֶל מִלֶּכֶת אֶל־בֵּית מִשְׁתֶּה בַּאֲשֶׁר הוּא סוֹף כָּל־הָאָדָם וְהַחַי
יִתֵּן אֶל־לִבּוֹ: ג טוֹב כַּעַס מִשְּׂחֹק כִּי־בְרֹעַ פָּנִים יִיטַב לֵב: ד לֵב חֲכָמִים
בְּבֵית אֵבֶל וְלֵב כְּסִילִים בְּבֵית שִׂמְחָה:

7 ¹ Better a good reputation than good oil[a]
and the day of death than the day of one's birth.

a. The Hebrew puns itself and is possibly a common aphorism, i.e., "reputation" (*shem*); "oil" (*shemen*). Good oil was a marked luxury (cf. II Kings 20:13). "Reputation" is also a

2 Better to go to a house of mourning than to a house of
    feasting;
for that is the end of every man, and he who is alive should
    take [it] to his heart.
3 Better vexation than laughter;
 for through a downcast[a] face, the heart is made better.[b]
4 The heart of wise men is in a house of mourning,
and the heart of dolts in a house of enjoyment.[c]

In one of the finest literary turns in Ecclesiastes, Kohelet, having just declared it impossible to know what is best to do in life, now proceeds to tell his reader what is better to do in life! This is less a contradiction than a reflection of his two commitments: to open-eyed observation and to finding a way to live. The structure is doubly effective in that the "better" things are presented, on one hand, as objectively superior, but at the same time they are reflective of Kohelet's thought – revelry is rejected, somber sobriety sought. The narrative thus moves assertively forward, but with advice that might make the reader consider whether he has in any way encountered a solution to the various frustrations observed to this point.

At this juncture Kohelet offers advice regarding superior attitudes and positions, almost all through comparisons. Articulated as proverbs, in a style typical of Wisdom literature, these are claims of truth, far from truisms. Interestingly, each piece of advice is worthy of independent consideration, and some of the points made might have been noted by other teachers – so much so that some commentators suggest that these verses were mostly quoted aphorisms. The format "X is better than Y" is well known from biblical Hebrew and international Wisdom literature. Kohelet used the form earlier not to give advice but rather to articulate observations (vv. 4:3, 6, 9, 13.)

In any case, the collected series of suggestions has a particularly heavy tone, befitting the opening turn to death for enlightenment. Kohelet "seems to have

bridge to the previous paragraph, being the same Hebrew word as "designated" in 6:10.
a. "Downcast" – the root, used often, implies "bad," increasing the irony of the end of the verse.
b. A type of joy – see the commentary.
c. "House of enjoyment" may be a then-familiar specific reference, such as a pub or the like, or a parallel to the house of feasting (which probably refers to a wedding celebration) in 7:2.

intended to administer a shock to his readers…through a sober recognition of human mortality,"[23] a necessary balance to his frequent recommendation of enjoyment, lest the recommendation be misunderstood.

Many of the aphorisms are open to interpretation. Verse 2 (the advice to go to a house of mourning), for example, can be seen as advice to learn what one will need at the time of death ("honor," Rashi; "a final good name," Sforno) or a warning to be aware of one's inevitable fate (Ibn Ezra). Verse 3 is literarily striking: a "downcast" face creating a "better" heart. This paragraph is particularly complex and challenging. A "good heart" indicates a certain kind of enjoyment, one often associated with drinking and feasting(!),[24] and Kohelet seems to be recommending arrival at this feeling through an acquaintance with death, resulting in a very sober delight, as it were, as opposed to gaining a "good heart" directly through the "house of feasting."

By way of overview of this paragraph: Kohelet to this point in chapter 7, having rejected common pursuits, opts instead for level-headed contemplation, and now continues in that mode.

ה:ז טוֹב לִשְׁמֹעַ גַּעֲרַת חָכָם מֵאִישׁ שֹׁמֵעַ שִׁיר כְּסִילִים׃ ו כִּי כְקוֹל הַסִּירִים תַּחַת הַסִּיר כֵּן שְׂחֹק הַכְּסִיל וְגַם־זֶה הָבֶל׃ ז כִּי הָעֹשֶׁק יְהוֹלֵל חָכָם וִיאַבֵּד אֶת־לֵב מַתָּנָה׃

> 7:5 Better listening to a wise man's reproof
> than that a man listen to the singing of dolts,
> 6 for the laughter of the dolt is like
> the sound of nettles under a kettle[a] –
> but this, too, is vapor,[b]
> 7 for extortion may drive a wise man to depravity,
> and a bribe may subdue the heart.

The pieces of advice continue to flow smoothly by association, with Kohelet's overview of life still strongly reflected. He prefers wisdom, but in a quick

a. English reproduces an echo in the Hebrew – i.e., "nettles" (*sirim*); "kettle" (*sir*) – possibly a well-known phrase (according to Barton). "Singing" (*shir*), verse 5, can also be echoed by "kettle" (*sir*). Note that nettles burn at a low temperature, so their heat is relatively ineffective (according to Rashbam). Additionally, such a flame quickly burns itself out (Kara).
b. Vapor is a double reference: to the example (the ineffective sound of the nettles) and to the reliance on the wise, which, even though recommended, is only of fleeting import.

and fascinating reversal, he refuses to do so wholeheartedly, for wisdom is corruptible. Indeed, there are many biblical statements indicating that bribes and self-concern can undermine wisdom and/or righteousness.[a]

זח טוֹב אַחֲרִית דָּבָר מֵרֵאשִׁיתוֹ טוֹב אֶרֶךְ־רוּחַ מִגְּבַהּ־רוּחַ: ט אַל־
תְּבַהֵל בְּרוּחֲךָ לִכְעוֹס כִּי כַעַס בְּחֵיק כְּסִילִים יָנוּחַ: י אַל־תֹּאמַר מֶה הָיָה
שֶׁהַיָּמִים הָרִאשֹׁנִים הָיוּ טוֹבִים מֵאֵלֶּה כִּי לֹא מֵחָכְמָה שָׁאַלְתָּ עַל־זֶה:

7:8 Better the end of a matter than its beginning;
better a patient spirit than a haughty spirit.
9 Do not let your spirit hasten to vexation,
for vexation rests in the breast of dolts.
10 Do not say, "How is it that the former times were better than these?,"
for it is not wise of you to ask about this.

Kohelet goes on to say that patience is required in life. In terms of the apparent conflict between verse 9 and verse 3 above ("better vexation than laughter"), there vexation is preferable to idle laughter, whereas here it is of less value than patience. Note that verse 10 does not deny that the past may have been better, only that dwelling on the question is not advisable. These three sentences together advise a longer point of view and thus form an appropriate summary of the advice in chapter 7 to this point (so Kara).

זיא טוֹבָה חָכְמָה עִם־נַחֲלָה וְיֹתֵר לְרֹאֵי הַשָּׁמֶשׁ: יב כִּי בְּצֵל הַחָכְמָה
בְּצֵל הַכָּסֶף וְיִתְרוֹן דַּעַת הַחָכְמָה תְּחַיֶּה בְעָלֶיהָ:

7:11 Wisdom is good, just like an inheritance,
an advantage for those who see the sun,
12 for to be in the shadow of wisdom is to be in the shadow
of silver;
and the advantage of knowledge is that wisdom preserves
the life of its owner.

Kohelet continues to offer insights that could derive from other Wisdom teachers, even though he adds a cynical tone through the utilitarian justification.

a. Cf. Exod. 23:8; Deut.16:19; Jer. 22:17.

TAKE JOY – WHEN YOU CAN

יג רְאֵה אֶת־מַעֲשֵׂה הָאֱלֹהִים כִּי מִי יוּכַל לְתַקֵּן אֵת אֲשֶׁר עִוְּתוֹ: יד בְּיוֹם
טוֹבָה הֱיֵה בְטוֹב וּבְיוֹם רָעָה רְאֵה גַּם אֶת־זֶה לְעֻמַּת־זֶה עָשָׂה הָאֱלֹהִים
עַל־דִּבְרַת שֶׁלֹּא יִמְצָא הָאָדָם אַחֲרָיו מְאוּמָה:

7:13 See God's doing! Indeed, who can fix what He has twisted?[a] **14** On
a good day, experience the good life,[b] and on a bad day, see this: God
made one alongside the other, so that man might find nothing of what
[comes] after him.

At the end of Kohelet's advice, there is a surprising bitter cry, possibly reflecting his frustration, as his recommendation for sober, level-headed contemplation encounters his ultimate realization that he cannot understand it all
(v. 13). Up to this point in the text, Kohelet has not been wont to imply God's
responsibility for what he has (not) found in his search, and this verse seems
to be a peak of indirect accusation (already hinted at in 1:13 and 3:10–11).

Although he comes close to his former repeated references to enjoyment
by recommending "take delight" (a synonym for "enjoy"[25]), the framework
for his comments has emerged with a vengeance. The world is twisted and
unfathomable. When possible, then, one should appreciate and enjoy good
fortune, and when that is not possible, one must understand that one cannot
understand! Literarily, Kohelet ends the long segment of comparison (of
one thing "better" than another) in verse 14 with a rather powerless and
meaningless "good" and "bad" (apart from the implication that one should
not participate in the "bad").

The core term of section 3 is "good/better," accurately reflecting its second
half.

a. Kohelet here recalls 1:15.
b. Literally, "experience the beneficence [the good]," a parallel expression for "enjoy," as
in 2:1 (and see note there), and a play on the words "on a 'good' day."

Part II, Section 4
Lost at Seeing (7:15–8:15)

טו:אֶת־הַכֹּל רָאִיתִי בִּימֵי הֶבְלִי יֵשׁ צַדִּיק אֹבֵד בְּצִדְקוֹ וְיֵשׁ רָשָׁע מַאֲרִיךְ בְּרָעָתוֹ:

7:15 I have seen everything in my vaporous days: at times a righteous man perishes even though he is righteous, and at times a wicked man lives long even though he is evil.

As Kohelet continues his search, two subtleties seem to reflect his recent advice to concentrate on death and mourning (7:1–4): the mention of the occasional early death of the righteous and his striking opening application of "vaporous" to his own life.

In the first case, Kohelet re-encounters one of the ultimate questions facing any religion based on transcendent justice – the suffering of the righteous. However, his concern is not specifically theological, nor does it bear the pathos of suffering, as in Job. The observed occasional absence of fair recompense immediately becomes a datum in his search for how best to live life, and he continues with appropriate advice.

The second subtlety, his "vaporous" life, foreshadows this section's later development, which becomes ever more personal.

CONSEQUENT ADVICE

טז:אַל־תְּהִי צַדִּיק הַרְבֵּה וְאַל־תִּתְחַכַּם יוֹתֵר לָמָּה תִּשּׁוֹמֵם: יז אַל־תִּרְשַׁע הַרְבֵּה וְאַל־תְּהִי סָכָל לָמָּה תָמוּת בְּלֹא עִתֶּךָ: יח טוֹב אֲשֶׁר תֶּאֱחֹז בָּזֶה וְגַם־מִזֶּה אַל־תַּנַּח אֶת־יָדֶךָ כִּי־יְרֵא אֱלֹהִים יֵצֵא אֶת־כֻּלָּם: יט הַחָכְמָה תָּעֹז לֶחָכָם מֵעֲשָׂרָה שַׁלִּיטִים אֲשֶׁר הָיוּ בָּעִיר: כ כִּי אָדָם

אֵין צַדִּיק בָּאָרֶץ אֲשֶׁר יַעֲשֶׂה־טּוֹב וְלֹא יֶחֱטָא: כא גַּם לְכָל־הַדְּבָרִים
אֲשֶׁר יְדַבֵּרוּ אַל־תִּתֵּן לִבֶּךָ אֲשֶׁר לֹא־תִשְׁמַע אֶת־עַבְדְּךָ מְקַלְלֶךָ: כב כִּי
גַּם־פְּעָמִים רַבּוֹת יָדַע לִבֶּךָ אֲשֶׁר גַּם־אַתְּ [אַתָּה] קִלַּלְתָּ אֲחֵרִים:

7:16 Do not be overly righteous, and do not act the wise man to excess –
why should you be appalled? **17** Do not be overly wicked and do not
be a fool – why should you die before your time? **18** Better that you
hold onto the one without letting go of the other, for one who fears
God will do his duty[26] by both.

    19 Wisdom fortifies the wise man more than ten[27] oligarchs[a] of the
city, **20** though there is no man so righteous[b] on earth that he does
good and never fails.

    21 Also, do not allow your heart to give [heed] to all words spoken,
lest you hear your slave reviling you; **22** for your heart knows of the
many times that even you have reviled others.

For the first time in part II, Kohelet proceeds almost immediately to advice
rather than observation, which will, in turn, lead him in this section to a
somewhat staccato back-and-forth between the two. This also foreshadows
an ever growing emphasis on advice.

    In one of the more startling paragraphs in Ecclesiastes, here Kohelet
recommends no excess – neither of wickedness nor of righteousness – and
he even suggests a bit of each. This is less principle than resignation. As he
clarifies further on in this paragraph, no one can avoid all evil (a common biblical claim – cf. 1 Kings 8:46 [possibly the source of 7:20 here, as a paraphrase];
Ps. 143:2; Prov. 20:9), and therefore he is reduced to advising against excess.

    Here he also takes an additional step toward "fear of God," deriving from
the apparently arbitrary nature of God's working in this world, a striking
combination of a traditional piece of advice with a very nontraditional reason
(and see the commentary on 3:14). In turn, this leads to more advice: since
you will undertake some objectionable acts, you should not overreact to
others' failings – they are only like you (so Sforno).

a. Root indicates "authority, control, rule" (*sh-l-t*).
b. The equivalency wise-righteous is frequent in the Bible: "The mouth of the righteous
produces wisdom" (Prov. 10:31).

"For many times" are the first Hebrew words of verse 22, thus emphasizing that the addressee has little basis in his own life for disparaging others' failures.

BITTER EXPERIENCE

כג: כָּל־זֹה נִסִּיתִי בַחָכְמָה אָמַרְתִּי אֶחְכָּמָה וְהִיא רְחוֹקָה מִמֶּנִּי: כד רָחוֹק
מַה־שֶּׁהָיָה וְעָמֹק ׀ עָמֹק מִי יִמְצָאֶנּוּ: כה סַבּוֹתִי אֲנִי וְלִבִּי לָדַעַת וְלָתוּר
וּבַקֵּשׁ חָכְמָה וְחֶשְׁבּוֹן וְלָדַעַת רֶשַׁע כֶּסֶל וְהַסִּכְלוּת הוֹלֵלוֹת:

7:23 All this I tested with wisdom. I said "I would be wise," but it is distant from me. **24** Distant is that which has happened, the deepest depth – who can find it? **25** So I turned, I and[a] my heart, to knowing – and probing and seeking – wisdom and calculation; and to knowing that wickedness is stupidity, foolishness is depravity![b]

Verse 24 nicely combines two metaphors, distance and depth. In verse 25 the author, well into part II's amalgam of Kohelet's observations and advice, chooses to bind the book closer together, as for the first time Kohelet frames these in terms similar to those of part I (compare this paragraph with 1:13, 16, 17 and 2:3, 12). In any case, here personal passion grows – to whatever degree Kohelet's insights were formerly dispassionate, here they are reframed as further elements of a personal search, as the reader can now clearly understand that the opening tale (the pseudo-autobiography) closely reflects the teacher Kohelet in the subsequent chapters. Retrospectively, this reinforces the personal use of "vaporous" in 7:15.

This personal involvement begins to explain Kohelet's presumably conflicting claims that he had achieved wisdom (as in part I) or could not achieve it (as seen here). He clearly has learned a great deal, and so he shares. He has not, however, accomplished his goal of finding empirical knowledge to verify the traditions he has received. This leads not to a rejection of one or the other, but to frustration.[c]

כו: וּמוֹצֶא אֲנִי מַר מִמָּוֶת אֶת־הָאִשָּׁה אֲשֶׁר־הִיא מְצוֹדִים וַחֲרָמִים לִבָּהּ

a. "And my heart" is probably to be read "in my heart" as in many manuscripts (in 79 according to Crenshaw's count) and in some ancient translations.
b. This last phrase also can be read as "knowing wickedness, stupidity, and foolishness, depravity."
c. For the view that wisdom is discoverable, see Proverbs 8:17, 35.

אֲסוּרִים יָדֶיהָ טוֹב לִפְנֵי הָאֱלֹהִים יִמָּלֵט מִמֶּנָּה וְחוֹטֵא יִלָּכֶד בָּהּ: כז רְאֵה
זֶה מָצָאתִי אָמְרָה קֹהֶלֶת אַחַת לְאַחַת לִמְצֹא חֶשְׁבּוֹן: כח אֲשֶׁר עוֹד־
בִּקְשָׁה נַפְשִׁי וְלֹא מָצָאתִי אָדָם אֶחָד מֵאֶלֶף מָצָאתִי וְאִשָּׁה בְכָל־אֵלֶּה
לֹא מָצָאתִי: כט לְבַד רְאֵה־זֶה מָצָאתִי אֲשֶׁר עָשָׂה הָאֱלֹהִים אֶת־הָאָדָם
יָשָׁר וְהֵמָּה בִקְשׁוּ חִשְּׁבֹנוֹת רַבִּים:

7:26 Now I find more bitter than death that woman[a] who is all traps –
her heart is snares and her hands are fetters. One who is good[b] in God's
sight escapes her, and a failure is caught by her. **27** See, this I have found,
said Kohelet,[c] [adding] one to one[d] to find the calculation. **28** As for
what I[e] sought further but did not find: I found one man in a thousand,
and could not find a woman among all of them. **29** See, only this I
found: God made men plain, but they[f] have sought many calculations.

Kohelet is evidently swept along by his personal reflections to turn to what
would otherwise be a totally different subject. Indeed, the paragraph includes
half (seven) of Ecclesiastes's use of the term "find," a hint at more direct
experience.[g]

 This paragraph, along with his occasional references to not knowing his
heir, probably affords yet another insight into Kohelet's personal history – he
was likely not married and had no children. This conclusion is bolstered by a
pun in verse 28, for "to find a woman" often means "to find a wife."[28]

a. "That woman" might imply "womankind." One suspects that the overlapping meanings
reflect specific experience leading to the generalization.
b. That is, favored.
c. The narrator exceptionally is mentioned here, in the middle of the book for unclear
reasons. On the phrase "said Kohelet," see Review Essays 4.1A.
d. "One to one" implies "step by step," with a possible hint, by punning, of multiple attempts
to find a worthy woman. ("One" is feminine.)
e. "I," *nafshi*, is literally "my throat" (at times implying life breath, appetite, and inner being),
and it is used elsewhere in Ecclesiastes exclusively to indicate "appetites" (i.e., desires), a
possible subtle reference here to a physical relationship.
f. "They" (*heima*) is usually masculine, but sometimes feminine (Ruth 1:22; Zech. 5:10;
Song 6:8), so implying either that women (not men) are too calculating or that all males
are such (when looking for a woman) or all people are (in all matters – referring back to
7:23–24) – or all three! (The word "men" in this verse could imply either males or people.)
g. Elsewhere Kohelet generally uses the word "find" in reference to what is impossible to
apprehend, that is, what he cannot find. The term also appears in verse 24 immediately above.

The implied criticism of "many calculations" in verse 29 ironically reflects on verse 27, where the speaker does the calculating! This is another hint that these verses reflect personal failure, not objective observation.

FURTHER ADVICE

ח א מִי־כְּהֶחָכָם וּמִי יוֹדֵעַ פֵּשֶׁר דָּבָר חָכְמַת אָדָם תָּאִיר פָּנָיו וְעֹז
פָּנָיו יְשֻׁנֶּא: ב אֲנִי פִּי־מֶלֶךְ שְׁמֹר וְעַל דִּבְרַת שְׁבוּעַת אֱלֹהִים:
ג אַל־תִּבָּהֵל מִפָּנָיו תֵּלֵךְ אַל־תַּעֲמֹד בְּדָבָר רָע כִּי כָּל־אֲשֶׁר יַחְפֹּץ יַעֲשֶׂה:
ד בַּאֲשֶׁר דְּבַר־מֶלֶךְ שִׁלְטוֹן וּמִי יֹאמַר־לוֹ מַה־תַּעֲשֶׂה: ה שׁוֹמֵר מִצְוָה
לֹא יֵדַע דָּבָר רָע וְעֵת וּמִשְׁפָּט יֵדַע לֵב חָכָם:

8 ¹ Who is like the wise man, and who knows the interpretation of a saying:²⁹

a man's wisdom illuminates his face,

and the severity of his face is transformed?

2 I.ᵃ Abide by the [words of] the king's mouth, that, according to God's oath. 3 Do not be terrified, leave his presence; do not stand [insistent] in a bad matter, for whatever he desires, he does, 4 since a king's word is [total] authority. Thus who can say to him, "What are you doing?" 5 One who abides by a command will know no harm.ᵇ and the wise heart will know of judgment time.ᶜ

Returning to advice, Kohelet resumes the role of the wise teacher, and he now proceeds from subject to subject, each one repeating a term or terms from the preceding paragraph. He ultimately returns to the question that opened the section, the apparent lack of appropriate recompense for the righteous and the wicked.

Verses 1 and 2 are difficult. As translated here, Kohelet claims that he understands the truth behind an accepted principle, which is that one should act

a. A unique structure, possibly meaning "I do," or "I say" – that is, the following is my understanding of the previous advice. The early versions do not translate "I," possibly reflecting that it was a later (and possibly accidental) addition.
b. "No harm" is literally "no bad thing" identical to "a bad matter" in verse 3, the root word for "harm" and "bad" representing the term used elsewhere for "evil" or "calamity."
c. A hendiadys, "time-and-judgment," indicating that he knows it exists, but not when it will happen (which would be the "time of judgment").

with caution in the presence of the powerful, smiling at the right time, staying when appropriate and leaving when necessary. (One should recall that at this time there was no king in Israel. The nature of these sayings, based in many centuries of Wisdom literature, is to make a principled point, not a specific guide for a specific moment. Further, the conceit of the book is that it comes from much earlier times.) The guiding principle is getting along with arbitrary power. (Various interpretations and emendations of verse 3 emphasize one tactic or another, some reading the two first phrases as the two options: "do not rush to leave his presence, and do not stand [insistent] … etc." In any case, the point is to react cleverly in light of the king's absolute power.)

The advice to obey the king is found frequently in Wisdom literature. The "oath" (8.2) is either God's pledge to the king or the people's loyalty oath, in God's name, to obey the king.

The last phrase of the paragraph might have been meant to recall the time of judgment in 3:17, which is divine, not human. Thus the paragraph becomes a grand bivalency, applying to king and/or "King." (Indeed, Isaiah 45:9 and Job 9:12 use language parallel to 8.4 to indicate that one cannot challenge God. Rashbam applies this whole paragraph to God exclusively.) If "King" (i.e., the Deity) is understood (by itself or as part of a bivalency), this would be yet another radical step in articulating Kohelet's fear of a distant, powerful, and apparently (from a human standpoint) arbitrary God.

ח:ו כִּי לְכָל־חֵפֶץ יֵשׁ עֵת וּמִשְׁפָּט כִּי־רָעַת הָאָדָם רַבָּה עָלָיו: ז כִּי־אֵינֶנּוּ
יֹדֵעַ מַה־שֶּׁיִּהְיֶה כִּי כַּאֲשֶׁר יִהְיֶה מִי יַגִּיד לוֹ: ח אֵין אָדָם שַׁלִּיט בָּרוּחַ
לִכְלוֹא אֶת־הָרוּחַ וְאֵין שִׁלְטוֹן בְּיוֹם הַמָּוֶת וְאֵין מִשְׁלַחַת בַּמִּלְחָמָה
וְלֹא־יְמַלֵּט רֶשַׁע אֶת־בְּעָלָיו:

8:6 Indeed, there is a judgment time for every pursuit;[a] indeed, a man's calamity overwhelms him; **7** indeed, he does not know what is to occur; indeed, who can tell him when it is to occur? **8** No man has control over the spirit, to retain the spirit: so that there is no authority over the day of death, and there is no mustering out from that war, and wickedness cannot save its practitioners.[b]

a. For an explanation of the translation, see the note on 3:1.
b. Translation and reference of the last two phrases are uncertain. The translation follows Barton and others on "mustering out" (often "furlough") and assumes that the elements of the verse are directly connected.

"Judgment time" leads Kohelet to another reflection. He begins to move in on the irresolvable conflict of empirical evidence and known traditional truth, with an insistent echo of four uses of "indeed" (vv. 6–7) to be echoed by four negatives (v. 8). There is a judgment time, but it is unknown, it is overpowering, and no one can influence its timing. Verse 7 is particularly powerful in its incongruity. Verse 8 focuses on the ultimate negative fate, death, the final phrase possibly reflecting desperate attempts to seize upon anything that might avoid it.

ח:ט אֶת־כָּל־זֶה רָאִ֫יתִי וְנָת֥וֹן אֶת־לִבִּ֗י לְכָל־מַעֲשֶׂה אֲשֶׁר נַעֲשָׂה תַּ֫חַת הַשֶּׁמֶשׁ עֵת אֲשֶׁר שָׁלַ֫ט הָאָדָ֥ם בְּאָדָ֖ם לְרַ֖ע לֽוֹ: י וּבְכֵ֗ן רָאִ֫יתִי רְשָׁעִ֜ים קְבֻרִ֥ים וָבָ֗אוּ וּמִמְּק֥וֹם קָד֖וֹשׁ יְהַלֵּ֗כוּ וְיִשְׁתַּכְּח֥וּ בָעִ֖יר אֲשֶׁ֥ר כֵּן־עָשׂ֑וּ גַּם־זֶ֥ה הָֽבֶל:

8:9 All this I saw, leading my heart to [see] every deed done under sun, at a time when one man has authority over another man to his detriment; **10** and then, I saw evildoers brought to burial, coming from the Holy Site, while such as had acted properly[a] were forgotten in the city.[b] This too is vapor.

These two verses seem to reflect, respectively, the two previous paragraphs, verse 9 bemoaning the power of one person over another (continuing vv. 1–5) and verse 10, though admittedly garbled (see the note), going one step beyond the death in verses 6–9, to the funeral. Two views of life's inequities, the verses hint ("then," v. 10) at a unifying story – either the man in authority of the first verse is among those buried with pomp in the second, or he is the one who orders that burial.

REPRISE: NO LOGIC TO REWARD AND PUNISHMENT

ח:יא אֲשֶׁ֨ר אֵין־נַעֲשָׂ֜ה פִתְגָם מַעֲשֵׂ֤ה הָרָעָה מְהֵרָ֑ה עַל־כֵּ֗ן מָלֵ֛א לֵ֥ב בְּנֵֽי־הָאָדָ֥ם בָּהֶ֖ם לַעֲשׂ֥וֹת רָֽע: יב אֲשֶׁ֨ר חֹטֶ֜א עֹשֶׂ֥ה רַ֛ע מְאַ֖ת וּמַאֲרִ֣יךְ ל֑וֹ כִּ֣י גַּם־יוֹדֵ֣עַ אָ֗נִי אֲשֶׁ֤ר יִהְיֶה־טּוֹב לְיִרְאֵ֣י הָֽאֱלֹהִ֔ים אֲשֶׁ֥ר יִֽירְא֖וּ מִלְּפָנָֽיו: יג וְטוֹב֙ לֹא־יִהְיֶ֣ה לָֽרָשָׁ֔ע וְלֹֽא־יַאֲרִ֤יךְ יָמִים֙ כַּצֵּ֔ל אֲשֶׁ֛ר אֵינֶ֥נּוּ יָרֵ֖א מִלִּפְנֵ֥י

a. See II Kings 7:9 for a parallel use of this terminology.

b. Verse 10 is uncertain. All versions and commentaries reflect significant confusion. Possibly, after "Site," read, "and how they acted was forgotten in the city."

אֱלֹהִים: יד יֶשׁ־הֶבֶל אֲשֶׁר נַעֲשָׂה עַל־הָאָרֶץ אֲשֶׁר ׀ יֵשׁ צַדִּיקִים אֲשֶׁר
מַגִּיעַ אֲלֵהֶם כְּמַעֲשֵׂה הָרְשָׁעִים וְיֵשׁ רְשָׁעִים שֶׁמַּגִּיעַ אֲלֵהֶם כְּמַעֲשֵׂה
הַצַּדִּיקִים אָמַרְתִּי שֶׁגַּם־זֶה הָבֶל:

8:11 As to the sentence for an evil deed not being carried out quickly, for which reason man's heart is full set to do evil; **12** [and] as to one who is a failure doing evil a hundred times but surviving long – indeed even so I know that it will be well with those who fear God in that they fear in His presence, **13** and it will not be well with the wicked one, and, like a shadow, he will not live long, because he does not fear in God's presence. **14** There is vapor [in] that which is done on earth, that there are righteous people who are requited according to the conduct of the wicked, and there are wicked ones who are requited according to the conduct of the righteous. And I say: all this, too, is vapor.

Observation has led back to considering delayed or inappropriate recompense for behavior, the subject with which Kohelet began this section. This paragraph is inherently conflicted, and some commentators "solve" this by assuming that verses 12 and 13 represent accepted truths (or aphorisms), which, based on experience, Kohelet goes on to deny. The plain text, however, is that Kohelet accepts both sources of truth.

The "vapor" used twice in verse 14 does not indicate evil or ridiculousness ("absurdity"), but rather something that cannot be grasped, in time or in space, and the observed world is termed "vapor" just as are the initial traditional assumptions about the world. The opening of the verse is masterfully dramatic, for to declare "there is vapor" borders on being an oxymoron, for vapor is precisely that which does not have substance in place or time. The phrase is striking in the extreme,[a] almost a screaming out, for which the echo "this is … vapor" at the end of the same verse is a reconfirmation. Kohelet is seemingly reacting to his own momentary drift into a traditional stance (vv. 12b–13).

---

a. There is no parallel use of "there is" with "vapor" in the Bible.

THE ONLY OPTION: TO ENJOY

ח:טו וְשִׁבַּחְתִּי אֲנִי אֶת־הַשִּׂמְחָה אֲשֶׁר אֵין־טוֹב לָאָדָם תַּחַת הַשֶּׁמֶשׁ כִּי
אִם־לֶאֱכֹל וְלִשְׁתּוֹת וְלִשְׂמוֹחַ וְהוּא יִלְוֶנּוּ בַעֲמָלוֹ יְמֵי חַיָּיו אֲשֶׁר־נָתַן־לוֹ
הָאֱלֹהִים תַּחַת הַשָּׁמֶשׁ׃

8:15 So I, I commended enjoyment, to this effect: there is nothing better
under the sun for a man than to eat, to drink, and to be joyful, and
that can accompany him, in exchange for the fruits of his toil, during
the days of life that God grants him under the sun.

Once again Kohelet returns to the one partial solution – enjoying what one
can. One also hears ever more strongly the resignation. This is the solution
with which one is left, all else having proved to be vapor.

This section differs from previous ones in part II by hinting at a broad basis
of direct experience rather than observation (hence the relatively sparse use
of the key word "see," with only four appearances). Hints include the phrase
"my vaporous days," the references to the early autobiography (see 7:23–25,
and note his egocentricity – if he failed, then no one can be wise!); the
possible autobiographical basis of 7:26–29; "I" in 8:2; and "even so I know"
in 8:12. The core term of the section, "find/discover," reflects the grounding
in personal experience.

Part II, Section 5

Toward Love and Life (8:16–9:10)

IN THE HANDS OF GOD

ח:טז כַּאֲשֶׁר נָתַתִּי אֶת־לִבִּי לָדַעַת חָכְמָה וְלִרְאוֹת אֶת־הָעִנְיָן אֲשֶׁר נַעֲשָׂה
עַל־הָאָרֶץ כִּי גַם בַּיּוֹם וּבַלַּיְלָה שֵׁנָה בְּעֵינָיו אֵינֶנּוּ רֹאֶה: יז וְרָאִיתִי אֶת־
כָּל־מַעֲשֵׂה הָאֱלֹהִים כִּי לֹא יוּכַל הָאָדָם לִמְצוֹא אֶת־הַמַּעֲשֶׂה אֲשֶׁר
נַעֲשָׂה תַחַת־הַשֶּׁמֶשׁ בְּשֶׁל אֲשֶׁר יַעֲמֹל הָאָדָם לְבַקֵּשׁ וְלֹא יִמְצָא וְגַם
אִם־יֹאמַר הֶחָכָם לָדַעַת לֹא יוּכַל לִמְצֹא:

8:16 When I applied my heart to know wisdom and to see the concerns carried out on earth – even to the extent of one's eyes seeing sleep neither day nor night – **17** then I saw all of God's deed(s): indeed, man cannot comprehend[a] those deeds, as done under the sun, in that what man toils to seek, he does not find; and even if a wise man intends[b] to know, he cannot find.

Kohelet echoes the terminology of 8:14 (there "done," the same Hebrew as verse 17's "carried out"), now adding to his conclusion there (i.e., that all is vapor) a reflection of his physical weariness for the task he has undertaken, giving the reader another personal insight into his character. As he progresses through the long middle unit, the term "see," which opens all the sections, appears here three times in the beginning, one use ("see sleep") graphically clarifying the use of "see" as "experience." The effort to see seems to have been without limit (day and night).

a. "Comprehend" is the term "find" (*m-ts-'*) in the rest of the verse, and throughout the book. Here, all three imply "grasp." "Concerns" and "deeds" in this paragraph are collective nouns indicating all of the acts together.
b. Or "expects."

"All of God's deeds" (v. 17) – Kohelet claims that there is no discernible encompassing principle that lies behind what happens. Verse 17 echoes 3:11, the conclusion of part 1, thus continuing (and now ending) the emphasis of the previous section (7:15–8:15) on knowledge drawn from personal experience.

ט א כִּי אֶת־כָּל־זֶה נָתַתִּי אֶל־לִבִּי וְלָבוּר אֶת־כָּל־זֶה אֲשֶׁר הַצַּדִּיקִים וְהַחֲכָמִים וַעֲבָדֵיהֶם בְּיַד הָאֱלֹהִים גַּם־אַהֲבָה גַּם־שִׂנְאָה אֵין יוֹדֵעַ הָאָדָם הַכֹּל לִפְנֵיהֶם: ב הַכֹּל כַּאֲשֶׁר לַכֹּל מִקְרֶה אֶחָד לַצַּדִּיק וְלָרָשָׁע לַטּוֹב וְלַטָּהוֹר וְלַטָּמֵא וְלַזֹּבֵחַ וְלַאֲשֶׁר אֵינֶנּוּ זֹבֵחַ כַּטּוֹב כַּחֹטֶא הַנִּשְׁבָּע כַּאֲשֶׁר שְׁבוּעָה יָרֵא: ג זֶה ׀ רָע בְּכֹל אֲשֶׁר־נַעֲשָׂה תַּחַת הַשֶּׁמֶשׁ כִּי־מִקְרֶה אֶחָד לַכֹּל וְגַם לֵב בְּנֵי־הָאָדָם מָלֵא־רָע וְהוֹלֵלוֹת בִּלְבָבָם בְּחַיֵּיהֶם וְאַחֲרָיו אֶל־הַמֵּתִים: ד כִּי־מִי אֲשֶׁר יְבֻחַר [יְחֻבַּר] אֶל כָּל־הַחַיִּים יֵשׁ בִּטָּחוֹן כִּי־לְכֶלֶב חַי הוּא טוֹב מִן־הָאַרְיֵה הַמֵּת: ה כִּי הַחַיִּים יוֹדְעִים שֶׁיָּמֻתוּ וְהַמֵּתִים אֵינָם יוֹדְעִים מְאוּמָה וְאֵין־עוֹד לָהֶם שָׂכָר כִּי נִשְׁכַּח זִכְרָם: ו גַּם אַהֲבָתָם גַּם־שִׂנְאָתָם גַּם־קִנְאָתָם כְּבָר אָבָדָה וְחֵלֶק אֵין־לָהֶם עוֹד לְעוֹלָם בְּכֹל אֲשֶׁר־נַעֲשָׂה תַּחַת הַשָּׁמֶשׁ:

9 1 Indeed, all of this – I allowed my heart to test all of this, how the righteous and the wise and their dealings are in the hand of God. Even love! Even hate! Man does not know – anything may be facing them, **2** anything, which is the case for anyone,[a] one destiny for the righteous and for the wicked; for the good and for the pure and for the impure; and for him who sacrifices and for him who does not sacrifice; the good one is like the one who is a failure; one who takes oaths like one who fears taking oaths.[b] **3** This is an evil within all that is done under the sun: that everyone has one destiny. Moreover, the heart of humanity is full of evil, with depravity in their heart while they live; as his future is – to the dead![c] **4** Yet he who is among[30] all

a. The verse implies "uncertainty for everybody."
b. Fearing oaths possibly implies guilt, as in Roland de Vaux, *Ancient Israel* (New York: McGraw Hill, 1961), p. 15.
c. Rashbam understands "as his future is – to the dead" as the thought of depraved humanity, approximately, "[After all,] one's end is to die."

the living has some security[a] – even a live dog[b] is better off than a dead lion – **5** for the living know they will die, but the dead know nothing; they have no more reward, indeed, their memory has been forgotten. **6** Even their love, even their hate, and even their jealousy is already lost, and for eternity they have no further portion in all that is done under the sun.

<u>Even the wise and the righteous cannot determine their lot.</u> As the uniform fate of all humankind weighs upon Kohelet, he is moved to revise his earlier observations. Unambiguously, he now finds life superior to death (compare his statements in 4:2; 6:3; and 7:1). Prior to this time, he had wondered if death were not preferable. He now sees the finality and total vacuum of death as the ultimate horror, dramatized by the blunt ending of verse 3. In restating that below (v. 10) he further emphasizes that death holds no possible hope (as opposed to 3:21, where this remained a question).

"Love" and "hate" in 9:1 evidently refer to the receipt thereof (from God, or from other humans). These are balanced, by way of closure, with the subject's love and hate toward others, in verse 6. (Love and hate evidently form a merism for all deep emotions.)

Verse 4b may cite a popular aphorism ("even a live dog…"), but in any case, Kohelet adds the depth of the effect of death in verse 5. Note also the power and finality of the phrase in verse 5, where even "memory" is "forgotten." In Hebrew, three terms in verse 6 rhyme: "their love" (*ahavatam*), "their hate" (*sinatam*), "their jealousy" (*kinatam*). They also rhyme with the word "even" (*gam*), which introduces each one. This rhyme scheme reinforces the all-embracing nature of the loss, as does the assonance between "reward" (*sachar*) and "memory" (*zeicher*) in verse 5 (possibly a proverbial description of what is absent in death).

AN EXTENDED PRAISE OF ENJOYMENT, IN THE SHADOW OF DEATH

טו לֵךְ אֱכֹל בְּשִׂמְחָה לַחְמֶךָ וּשֲׁתֵה בְלֶב־טוֹב יֵינֶךָ כִּי כְבָר רָצָה הָאֱלֹהִים אֶת־מַעֲשֶׂיךָ: ח בְּכָל־עֵת יִהְיוּ בְגָדֶיךָ לְבָנִים וְשֶׁמֶן עַל־רֹאשְׁךָ אַל־יֶחְסָר:

a. "Security" is from a root meaning "trust," though the continuation scarcely justifies the translation "certainty," which some suggest.

b. Dogs were viewed negatively in most biblical references, both wild (as a symbol of scavenging, eating corpses, e.g., I Kings 14:11) and domesticated (as a symbol of inferiority: cf. I Sam. 17:43; II Kings 8:13).

ט רְאֵה חַיִּים עִם־אִשָּׁה אֲשֶׁר־אָהַבְתָּ כָּל־יְמֵי חַיֵּי הֶבְלֶךָ אֲשֶׁר נָתַן־לְךָ
תַּחַת הַשֶּׁמֶשׁ כֹּל יְמֵי הֶבְלֶךָ כִּי הוּא חֶלְקְךָ בַּחַיִּים וּבַעֲמָלְךָ אֲשֶׁר־אַתָּה
עָמֵל תַּחַת הַשָּׁמֶשׁ: י כֹּל אֲשֶׁר תִּמְצָא יָדְךָ לַעֲשׂוֹת בְּכֹחֲךָ עֲשֵׂה כִּי אֵין
מַעֲשֶׂה וְחֶשְׁבּוֹן וְדַעַת וְחָכְמָה בִּשְׁאוֹל אֲשֶׁר אַתָּה הֹלֵךְ שָׁמָּה:

9:7 Go, eat your bread in joy, and drink your wine with good heart,[a] for God already has approved your actions. **8** At all times let your clothes be white, and may your head never be lacking oil. **9** Experience[b] life with a woman you love all the days of your vaporous life which He has granted you under the sun – all your vaporous days, for that is your portion in life and [the portion of] the spoils for which you toil under the sun. **10** Whatever your hand finds possible to do with your might,[c] do, for there is no deed, calculation, knowledge, or wisdom in Sheol, to which you go.

In what feels like the pinnacle of his observations-and-advice, Kohelet, having dwelt on the ultimate unknown, turns to the one piece of advice that he has repeated most often: enjoy. However, he now uses imperative forms, whereas he previously had "observed" this advantage. He thus intensifies the recommendation of enjoyment. Furthermore, that advice is expanded here, detailed not only by way of breadth and detail – eating, drinking, dressing up, and marriage – but also by way of a final generalization: *whatever* you can achieve from your wealth (or power), enjoy (and the word "with your power/wealth" could be an adverb modifying what you can do or, alternatively, modifying the imperative "do" or both). God so desires! One could scarcely imagine greater emphasis. He also changes his preferred methodology. In verse 7:3 (see the commentary there) he reverses traditional wisdom, seeking joy in vexation, but now returns to seeking it in wine.

However, Kohelet could not let himself end with a positive. Death, which has so occupied him, is recalled here once more in all its finality. (Note the complete four categories of negatives in verse 9:10.) Three of the terms in

a. "Good heart" is a type of enjoyment or delight (cf. 7:3; 11:7) often associated with drinking. (See the note on 7:3.)
b. The term used throughout the book is "see," which often implies "experience."
c. Alternatively, "your wealth" (cf. Prov. 5:10; Job 6:22). Saadia Gaon interprets "while you have the power," and Rashbam, "while you live."

verse 10 ("calculation," "knowledge," and "wisdom") are personal, reflections of his own lifelong search.

The core term of section 5 is "life/living," reflecting Kohelet's newfound preference.

Part II, Section 6
Calculations, True and False (9:11–11:8)

KOHELET'S FINAL COLLECTION: EFFORTS AND SKILLS THAT LEAD
NOWHERE

At this point, Kohelet returns to one more cycle of observation and advice,
bringing part II to a close with selected recollections and reiterations. Having
declared that life is the preferred option, he now focuses on efforts that help
people get along, but dismisses them as only partially effective, at best. He
ends with a final repetition of the one principal desideratum – enjoyment.

יא: שַׁבְתִּי וְרָאֹה תַחַת־הַשֶּׁמֶשׁ כִּי לֹא לַקַּלִּים הַמֵּרוֹץ וְלֹא לַגִּבּוֹרִים
הַמִּלְחָמָה וְגַם לֹא לַחֲכָמִים לֶחֶם וְגַם לֹא לַנְּבֹנִים עֹשֶׁר וְגַם לֹא לַיֹּדְעִים
חֵן כִּי־עֵת וָפֶגַע יִקְרֶה אֶת־כֻּלָּם: יב כִּי גַּם לֹא־יֵדַע הָאָדָם אֶת־עִתּוֹ
כַּדָּגִים שֶׁנֶּאֱחָזִים בִּמְצוֹדָה רָעָה וְכַצִּפֳּרִים הָאֲחֻזוֹת בַּפָּח כָּהֵם יוּקָשִׁים
בְּנֵי הָאָדָם לְעֵת רָעָה כְּשֶׁתִּפּוֹל עֲלֵיהֶם פִּתְאֹם:

9:11 I have further seen under the sun that the race[a] is not won by[b] the
swift, and the battle is not won by the strong; so, too, bread is not won
by the wise; so, too, wealth is not won by the astute; so, too, favor is not
won by the knowledgeable, for unpredictability[c] is the destiny of all.
12 Indeed, a man cannot even[d] know his time. As fish are caught in a

a. The race here is probably connected to couriers rather than sport (as interpreted by
Crenshaw), despite the chosen translation "won by" (see the next note).
b. All parallel phrases in this verse literally read that X (the activity) does not "belong to" Y
(the type of person), here translated "won by." The absolute, hyperbolic denial is effective
in making the point, but really implies "necessarily won by."
c. Uncertain – literally "time and encounter," a hendiadys.
d. "Even" is the same Hebrew as "too" (three times) in 9:11, adding to the emphasis on
scope.

calamitous[a] net, and as birds are caught in a snare, so men are trapped at a time of calamity, when it suddenly falls upon them.

Now preferring life, Kohelet begins a series of observations and comments all leading to the conclusion that one should be wise (i.e., show understanding and patience), but still must have limited expectations. He begins (and will end again) with the emphasis on death that marks the second half of the book. The recurrent theme of this final section of observations-and-advice is that (many) specific efforts, preparations, and qualities are often of no avail.

גַּם־זֹה רָאִיתִי חָכְמָה תַּחַת הַשֶּׁמֶשׁ וּגְדוֹלָה הִיא אֵלָי: יד עִיר קְטַנָּה יג
וַאֲנָשִׁים בָּהּ מְעָט וּבָא־אֵלֶיהָ מֶלֶךְ גָּדוֹל וְסָבַב אֹתָהּ וּבָנָה עָלֶיהָ מְצוֹדִים
גְּדֹלִים: טו וּמָצָא בָהּ אִישׁ מִסְכֵּן חָכָם וּמִלַּט־הוּא אֶת־הָעִיר בְּחָכְמָתוֹ
וְאָדָם לֹא זָכַר אֶת־הָאִישׁ הַמִּסְכֵּן הַהוּא: טז וְאָמַרְתִּי אָנִי טוֹבָה חָכְמָה
מִגְּבוּרָה וְחָכְמַת הַמִּסְכֵּן בְּזוּיָה וּדְבָרָיו אֵינָם נִשְׁמָעִים: יז דִּבְרֵי חֲכָמִים
בְּנַחַת נִשְׁמָעִים מִזַּעֲקַת מוֹשֵׁל בַּכְּסִילִים: יח טוֹבָה חָכְמָה מִכְּלֵי קְרָב
וְחוֹטֶא אֶחָד יְאַבֵּד טוֹבָה הַרְבֵּה:

א זְבוּבֵי מָוֶת יַבְאִישׁ יַבִּיעַ שֶׁמֶן רוֹקֵחַ יָקָר מֵחָכְמָה מִכָּבוֹד סִכְלוּת ◀
מְעָט:

9:13 Also, this I saw, [an example of] wisdom under the sun, and it seemed great to me: **14** a little town, with few people in it; and a great king came to it, who surrounded it and built great siege works against it. **15** Now one found therein a poor wise man who saved[b] the town with his wisdom, but no man remembered that poor person. **16** So I, I said: Better wisdom than strength, but the wisdom of the poor man is scorned, and his words are not heeded.

17 Words spoken tranquilly by the wise are heeded more than those shouted by a ruler of dolts; **18** better wisdom than weapons – but just one who is a failure destroys much good.

10 **1** Dead flies turn a perfumer's oil fetid and fermented; a little folly outweighs wisdom and honor.

a. "Calamity" (calamitous) in this verse elsewhere implies "evil" or "bad," incorporating that tone here.
b. Some interpret "could have saved."

To demonstrate the vulnerability of wisdom's benefit, Kohelet offers a didactic (true or fictional) tale. He explains that the accepted principles we live by (such as the effect of wise words) are subject to external circumstances. In terms of literature, he plays off juxtapositions (little/great, single/many, king/poor man, and, ultimately, wise man/dolt), but ironically dismisses any suggested formula for success, as rules collapse. A touch of bad destroys much good.

Verses 17–18a seem to present well-accepted principles, which then are said to be subject to a fatal flaw, vulnerable to a smidgeon of the wrong ingredient.

יׄב לֵב חָכָם לִימִינוֹ וְלֵב כְּסִיל לִשְׂמֹאלוֹ׃ ג וְגַם־בַּדֶּרֶךְ כְּשֶׁהַסָּכָל [כְּשֶׁסָּכָל]
הֹלֵךְ לִבּוֹ חָסֵר וְאָמַר לַכֹּל סָכָל הוּא׃

> 10:2 A wise man's heart is to his right,[a]
> a dolt's heart is to his left.
> 3 Even when he walks on the way, a fool's heart is absent,[b]
> declaring[c] to everyone that he is a fool.

To compound the complexity, Kohelet still praises wisdom, certainly compared to foolishness. In verse 2, "right" implies support, "left," misfortune.

יׄד אִם־רוּחַ הַמּוֹשֵׁל תַּעֲלֶה עָלֶיךָ מְקוֹמְךָ אַל־תַּנַּח כִּי מַרְפֵּא יַנִּיחַ
חֲטָאִים גְּדוֹלִים׃ ה יֵשׁ רָעָה רָאִיתִי תַּחַת הַשָּׁמֶשׁ כִּשְׁגָגָה שֶׁיֹּצָא מִלִּפְנֵי
הַשַּׁלִּיט׃ ו נִתַּן הַסֶּכֶל בַּמְּרוֹמִים רַבִּים וַעֲשִׁירִים בַּשֵּׁפֶל יֵשֵׁבוּ׃ ז רָאִיתִי
עֲבָדִים עַל־סוּסִים וְשָׂרִים הֹלְכִים כַּעֲבָדִים עַל־הָאָרֶץ׃

10:4 If the ruler's[d] temper[e] flares up against you, do not quit your place; for calmness brings acquittal[f] for grave offenses. 5 There is an evil I have seen under the sun, indeed, a mistake emanating from one in authority: 6 folly is placed on the greatest heights, while rich men sit

---

a. The positive implication of "right" probably derived from most people being right-handed. The implication is found in other languages as well, as the English "right" (proper, just).

b. That is, he shows no common sense.

c. That is, by his actions.

d. Same term is translated as "oligarch" in 7:19. Root is "authority."

e. The term (*ruach*) translated elsewhere as "spirit" or "wind."

f. "Quit" and "acquit" reflect a similar echo in Hebrew (*tanach/yaniach*).

in a low place. **7** I have seen slaves on horseback, and nobles walking across the land like slaves.

Again, wise behavior (v. 4) is undermined, this time by the terrible choices of rulers. Wise men do not always rise within the system.[31]

Some commentators bridle at Kohelet's apparent sympathy for the rich in this paragraph and guess that this was his social class (as also reflected in the early pseudo-autobiography?). However, parallels to regret for this reversal of order are found elsewhere in Wisdom literature.[a] It may simply be an inherited cultural norm, and just as one need not conclude from 9:11 that Kohelet was an athlete or a warrior, so one need not conclude that he was an aristocrat.

יח חֹפֵר גּוּמָץ בּוֹ יִפּוֹל וּפֹרֵץ גָּדֵר יִשְּׁכֶנּוּ נָחָשׁ: ט מַסִּיעַ אֲבָנִים יֵעָצֵב
בָּהֶם בּוֹקֵעַ עֵצִים יִסָּכֶן בָּם: י אִם־קֵהָה הַבַּרְזֶל וְהוּא לֹא־פָנִים קִלְקַל
וַחֲיָלִים יְגַבֵּר וְיִתְרוֹן הַכְשֵׁיר חָכְמָה: יא אִם־יִשֹּׁךְ הַנָּחָשׁ בְּלוֹא־לָחַשׁ
וְאֵין יִתְרוֹן לְבַעַל הַלָּשׁוֹן: יב דִּבְרֵי פִי־חָכָם חֵן וְשִׂפְתוֹת כְּסִיל תְּבַלְּעֶנּוּ:
יג תְּחִלַּת דִּבְרֵי־פִיהוּ סִכְלוּת וְאַחֲרִית פִּיהוּ הוֹלֵלוּת רָעָה: יד וְהַסָּכָל
יַרְבֶּה דְבָרִים לֹא־יֵדַע הָאָדָם מַה־שֶׁיִּהְיֶה וַאֲשֶׁר יִהְיֶה מֵאַחֲרָיו מִי יַגִּיד
לוֹ: טו עֲמַל הַכְּסִילִים תְּיַגְּעֶנּוּ אֲשֶׁר לֹא־יָדַע לָלֶכֶת אֶל־עִיר:

10:8 He who digs a pit may fall into it;
he who breaks a fence may be bitten by a snake.
9 He who quarries stones may be hurt by them;
he who chops trees may be endangered by them.[b]
10 If the iron[c] has become dull
and he has not whetted the edge,
then he must exert more strength,
thus the advantage of preparation is wisdom's.[d]

a. Cf. Prov. 30:22.
b. The verbs in the last two sentences are in the imperfect, and could be translated into the English future ("will fall…, will be bitten…, etc.") again lending a hyperbolic, absolute tone to the verse (like 9:11), which literarily increases its power.
c. "Iron" means ax, as in II Kings 6:5.
d. The translation of verse 10 is uncertain, the last phrase in particular a matter of conjecture.

11 If the snake strikes harm before the charm,[a]
then there is no advantage to the trained enchanter.
12 The words from a wise man's mouth are favor,[b]
but a dolt's lips devour him:
13 the beginning of the words of his mouth – foolishness,
and the end of [the words of] his mouth – calamitous
depravity.
14 Yet the fool makes his words many – a man cannot know what will
be, and who can tell him what will be after that? **15** The toil of dolts
wearies them, so that he does not even know how to get to a town.[c]

Well-intentioned and theoretically useful efforts often lead nowhere or to
a result that is the opposite of the one intended, whether owing to chance,
incomplete preparation, incorrect timing, or the undermining presence of
a dolt's words. (Kohelet is careful to indicate that the dolt has no positive
worth – his role is only that of a spoiler.) Verses 8 and 9 are comprehensive:
two activities reflect initial disassembling and the other two create the building materials, yet all lead to possible harm.

Verse 14b–c, here a description of the dolt's babbling, echoes 8:7, a description of the world's functioning, thus retrospectively adding depth to the gloom
reflected in the earlier verse.

טז: אִי־לָךְ אֶרֶץ שֶׁמַּלְכֵּךְ נָעַר וְשָׂרַיִךְ בַּבֹּקֶר יֹאכֵלוּ: יז אַשְׁרֵיךְ אֶרֶץ
שֶׁמַּלְכֵּךְ בֶּן־חוֹרִים וְשָׂרַיִךְ בָּעֵת יֹאכֵלוּ בִּגְבוּרָה וְלֹא בַשְּׁתִי: יח בַּעֲצַלְתַּיִם
יִמַּךְ הַמְּקָרֶה וּבְשִׁפְלוּת יָדַיִם יִדְלֹף הַבָּיִת: יט לִשְׂחוֹק עֹשִׂים לֶחֶם וְיַיִן
יְשַׂמַּח חַיִּים וְהַכֶּסֶף יַעֲנֶה אֶת־הַכֹּל: כ גַּם בְּמַדָּעֲךָ מֶלֶךְ אַל־תְּקַלֵּל
וּבְחַדְרֵי מִשְׁכָּבְךָ אַל־תְּקַלֵּל עָשִׁיר כִּי עוֹף הַשָּׁמַיִם יוֹלִיךְ אֶת־הַקּוֹל
וּבַעַל הַכְּנָפַיִם [כְּנָפַיִם] יַגֵּיד דָּבָר:

10:16 Woe to you, O land, if your king is a lad and if your ministers

---

a. Literally, "if the snake bites prior to a spell." English approximates a rhyme in the Hebrew: "snake" (*nachash*) and "spell" (*lachash*).
b. This means "elicits favor" (according to Rashbam and many others).
c. The last phrase is variously interpreted. Fox suggests that "get to town" is an idiom indicating success, based on approximate Egyptian equivalents. Barton cites an English parallel: "He doesn't even know when to come in out of the rain."

dine in the morning! **17** Happy are you, O land, if your king is noble and your ministers dine at the proper time – to make them strong, not to make them drunk!

> **18** Owing to slothfulness the roof beam sags;
> owing to un-lifted hands, the house leaks.

19 They*ᵃ* prepare a banquet for laughter, wine making life an enjoyment, and money is an answer for everything.*ᵇ*

> **20** Do not revile a king even to yourself,
> do not revile a rich man even in your bedroom;
> for a bird of the heavens may carry the sound,
> and a winged creature may report the word.

The text goes on to say that if dolts happen not to undo good effort, there is always the corrupt political establishment. That observation is followed by another precaution: do not rush to correct the political situation. (The placement of the adage in verse 20 may have been in response to Kohelet's realizing that he just spoke the same way (so Fox, but Kara, on the other hand, believes that verse 19 is preparatory for verse 20, noting the kind of men that these are, thus strengthening the caution against reviling them). The end of verse 20 bolsters Kohelet's warnings that one is not in control – even in circumstances that one deems safe, "somehow" the secret escapes. (Two English parallels: "The walls have ears" and "A little bird told me.")

PLAY IT SAFE AND . . .

יא א שַׁלַּח לַחְמְךָ עַל־פְּנֵי הַמָּיִם כִּי־בְרֹב הַיָּמִים תִּמְצָאֶנּוּ: ב תֶּן־חֵלֶק
לְשִׁבְעָה וְגַם לִשְׁמוֹנָה כִּי לֹא תֵדַע מַה־יִּהְיֶה רָעָה עַל־הָאָרֶץ:
ג אִם־יִמָּלְאוּ הֶעָבִים גֶּשֶׁם עַל־הָאָרֶץ יָרִיקוּ וְאִם־יִפּוֹל עֵץ בַּדָּרוֹם וְאִם
בַּצָּפוֹן מְקוֹם שֶׁיִּפּוֹל הָעֵץ שָׁם יְהוּא: ד שֹׁמֵר רוּחַ לֹא יִזְרָע וְרֹאֶה בֶעָבִים
לֹא יִקְצוֹר: ה כַּאֲשֶׁר אֵינְךָ יוֹדֵעַ מַה־דֶּרֶךְ הָרוּחַ כַּעֲצָמִים בְּבֶטֶן הַמְּלֵאָה
כָּכָה לֹא תֵדַע אֶת־מַעֲשֵׂה הָאֱלֹהִים אֲשֶׁר יַעֲשֶׂה אֶת־הַכֹּל: ו בַּבֹּקֶר
זְרַע אֶת־זַרְעֶךָ וְלָעֶרֶב אַל־תַּנַּח יָדֶךָ כִּי אֵינְךָ יוֹדֵעַ אֵי זֶה יִכְשָׁר הֲזֶה
אוֹ־זֶה וְאִם־שְׁנֵיהֶם כְּאֶחָד טוֹבִים:

a. "They" evidently implies the denigrated ministers of verses 16 and 17.
b. Sforno takes the phrase to indicate that these are men accustomed to taking bribes.

11 1 Send your bread forth on the face of the waters, for after many days you may find it. 2 Give a portion to seven or even to eight,[a] for you cannot know what calamity will be on earth. 3 If the clouds are filled with rain, they empty themselves on the earth; and if a tree falls to the south or to the north, the tree will remain in the place of its fall. 4 One watching the wind will never sow, and one looking at the clouds will never reap. 5 Just as you do not know the path of the spirit into[32] the embryo in the pregnant womb,[b] so you will not know[c] the deeds of God, Who does everything. 6 In the morning sow your seed, and as evening approaches, do not hold back your hand, since you do not know which is going to succeed, this or that, or whether both are equally good.

The overriding advice of this paragraph is to exercise prudence and to vary one's options, and although these verses include insights one might find in another collection of wisdom, from Kohelet they are shadowed by a heavy cloud of resignation. The meta-message is not only prudence, but also its context: lack of knowledge and arbitrary results, with no control. Here the implication is clear: do not undertake meticulous efforts, for there is no sure reward for that kind of detailed calculation. Instead, increase your chances by diversifying your investments of time and wealth.

The opening metaphor is particularly powerful as a warning against calculating results, for there is no inherent or obvious worth in the literal action of tossing bread on water.[33] The exact implication of verse 1 (and with it, verse 2) is uncertain – among suggestions are varied investments, taking risks, giving charity, doing good deeds (even for strangers), and taking random action. More than one may be implied, as is the nature of metaphor. In fact, the attempt to find an exclusive reference diminishes the poetry. The end of verse 2 may imply that such behavior as a societal norm might benefit one if times turn bad.

Verse 1 has a certain assonance to it, "send your bread" doubling a syllable (*shlach lachmicha*), and "waters" and "days" (*mayim, yamim*) echoing and rhyming. Verse 3 seems to depict a certain uncontrollable inevitability, the

a. This is a biblical Hebrew usage involving ascending adjacent digits to indicate "some/several," a form also found in other Semitic languages.
b. Literally, "full belly," echoing the "full clouds" (v. 3). "Embryo" is literally "bones."
c. That is, foresee.

theme picked up by the verses that follow. In verses 4 and 5, the author puns, as "wind" of verse 4 is the same word as "spirit" of verse 5.

Much of this paragraph can be read as either poetry or prose.

...OPT FOR ENJOYMENT

יא:ז וּמָתוֹק הָאוֹר וְטוֹב לַעֵינַיִם לִרְאוֹת אֶת־הַשָּׁמֶשׁ: ח כִּי אִם־שָׁנִים
הַרְבֵּה יִחְיֶה הָאָדָם בְּכֻלָּם יִשְׂמָח וְיִזְכֹּר אֶת־יְמֵי הַחֹשֶׁךְ כִּי־הַרְבֵּה יִהְיוּ
כָּל־שֶׁבָּא הָבֶל:

11:7 But sweet is the light and how good it is for the eyes to see the sun! **8** Even if a man lives many years, let him take joy in them all, remembering the days of darkness, which will be many. All that is to come is vapor!

Once again, as at the end of all of the sections in part II, the final advice is to enjoy. There are two possible understandings of "darkness," and both may be implied. On one hand, it could symbolize the difficulties of the final stages of life, as it will in 12:2. On the other hand, it could emblematize death, given that the opposite, "see the sun," indicates "life," not "youth," and given the demand to take joy in "all" the years of life. Here death is only negative, and for the first time, Kohelet creates a final equation: just as everything under the sun is vapor, so too is anything that is to come after death.

The core term of section 6 is "wisdom," possibly a wry reflection on the caution advised. Perhaps that is all that is left of "wisdom"!

Kohelet's Words Part III

Death and Enjoyment (11:9–12:7)

Part III, Section 1

Take Joy When You Can, When Young

יא:ט שְׂמַ֨ח בָּח֜וּר בְּיַלְדוּתֶ֗יךָ וִֽיטִֽיבְךָ֤ לִבְּךָ֙ בִּימֵ֣י בְחוּרוֹתֶ֔ךָ וְהַלֵּךְ֙ בְּדַרְכֵ֣י לִבְּךָ֗ וּבְמַרְאֵ֣י עֵינֶ֑יךָ וְדָ֕ע כִּ֧י עַל־כָּל־אֵ֛לֶּה יְבִֽיאֲךָ֥ הָאֱלֹהִ֖ים בַּמִּשְׁפָּֽט: י וְהָסֵ֥ר כַּ֙עַס֙ מִלִּבֶּ֔ךָ וְהַעֲבֵ֥ר רָעָ֖ה מִבְּשָׂרֶ֑ךָ כִּֽי־הַיַּלְד֥וּת וְהַֽשַּׁחֲר֖וּת הָֽבֶל:

11:9 Take joy, O youth, in your earliest years, and let your heart be good to you in the days of your youth, and walk in your heart's paths and with what your eyes can see[a] (but[b] know that for all these, God will call you to judgment); **10** and banish vexation from your heart, and chase away calamity from your flesh, for early years and life's dawn[c] are vapor.

Here Kohelet, exceptionally, begins with the advice with which he has concluded each of the sections in part II: <u>find enjoyment while you can</u>. These two verses largely duplicate the two previous ones, and can be seen as a recapitulation that introduces the final poem (as presented) and/or a continuation of the end of the previous section, although the enclosing repetition of "days of your youth" in 11:9 and 12:1 argues for the division as presented here. (Note that the transition from part I to part II similarly included a bridging section, 3:10–15.)

The parenthetical thought ending 11:9 is interpreted either as a counter-contention and warning ("but," as translated) or as a re-emphasis by stating that this is God's will ("and" – see the note).

It is difficult to know whether Kohelet meant to contradict the Torah's

a. That is, very real pleasures, akin to "see" in 11:7 above, and the parallel phrase, 6:9. This phrase is the alternative to the "darkness," above, 11:8, and following, 12:2.
b. Or "and."
c. This is a unique biblical term. Alternative possibilities are "black hair" (as understood by Rashi and many others) and "vigor." (Hence the translation is uncertain, but the implication is not.)

prohibition "that you not follow your heart and eyes" (Num. 15:39). In part
I it seems that he acted in such a way when young (2:10). If so, this would, at
the end of the book, be the clearest digression from tradition, almost advice to
sow wild oats. (Rashi and Ibn Ezra understood the verbs in that way, although
both posit a conditional implication to the beginning of the verse – "*if* you
do follow heart and eyes," then punishment will surely come. This is most
certainly not the direct meaning of the text.)

　　This paragraph scans as either prose or poetry, with much parallelism, an
apt introduction to the eloquent poem that follows.

Part III, Section 2
The Song of Old Age and Death

יב א וּזְכֹר אֶת־בּוֹרְאֶיךָ בִּימֵי בְּחוּרֹתֶיךָ

12 1 So remember[a] your Creator[b] in the days of your youth,

As translated, this verse reinforces the parenthetical phrase in 11:9, but if the term translated "Creator" means rather "vitality" (see note), this is a reinforcement of the thrust of that paragraph as a whole. In any case, it introduces the final poem, a portrait of approaching death, the subject that has come to preoccupy Kohelet (cf. 8:6–8; 9:1–6, 10; and 11:8).

עַד אֲשֶׁר לֹא־יָבֹאוּ יְמֵי הָרָעָה וְהִגִּיעוּ שָׁנִים אֲשֶׁר תֹּאמַר אֵין־לִי בָהֶם חֵפֶץ: ב עַד אֲשֶׁר לֹא־תֶחְשַׁךְ הַשֶּׁמֶשׁ וְהָאוֹר וְהַיָּרֵחַ וְהַכּוֹכָבִים וְשָׁבוּ הֶעָבִים אַחַר הַגָּשֶׁם: ג בַּיּוֹם שֶׁיָּזֻעוּ שֹׁמְרֵי הַבַּיִת וְהִתְעַוְּתוּ אַנְשֵׁי הֶחָיִל וּבָטְלוּ הַטֹּחֲנוֹת כִּי מִעֵטוּ וְחָשְׁכוּ הָרֹאוֹת בָּאֲרֻבּוֹת: ד וְסֻגְּרוּ דְלָתַיִם בַּשּׁוּק בִּשְׁפַל קוֹל הַטַּחֲנָה וְיָקוּם לְקוֹל הַצִּפּוֹר וְיִשַּׁחוּ כָּל־בְּנוֹת הַשִּׁיר: ה גַּם מִגָּבֹהַּ יִרָאוּ וְחַתְחַתִּים בַּדֶּרֶךְ וְיָנֵאץ הַשָּׁקֵד וְיִסְתַּבֵּל הֶחָגָב וְתָפֵר הָאֲבִיּוֹנָה כִּי־הֹלֵךְ הָאָדָם אֶל־בֵּית עוֹלָמוֹ וְסָבְבוּ בַשּׁוּק הַסֹּפְדִים: ו עַד אֲשֶׁר לֹא־יֵרָחֵק [יֵרָתֵק] חֶבֶל הַכֶּסֶף וְתָרֻץ גֻּלַּת הַזָּהָב וְתִשָּׁבֶר כַּד עַל־הַמַּבּוּעַ וְנָרֹץ הַגַּלְגַּל אֶל־הַבּוֹר: ז וְיָשֹׁב הֶעָפָר עַל־הָאָרֶץ כְּשֶׁהָיָה וְהָרוּחַ תָּשׁוּב אֶל־הָאֱלֹהִים אֲשֶׁר נְתָנָהּ:

before those days of calamity come
and those years arrive
of which you will say, "I have no desire for them"–

a. That is, "be mindful of."
b. Might mean "vitality," based on later rabbinic use of this root.

85

2 before the sun grows dark
– and the light and the moon and the stars –
and the clouds return after the rain;
3 on that day when the guards of the house tremble;
and the men of valor are bent;
and the ones*a* that grind, having become few, are idle;
and those that see through the windows grow dim;
4 and the portals in the market-street are shut –
as the sound of the grinding-mill grows fainter,
and one rises at the sound*b* of the bird,
and all the singers*c* of song are brought low;*d*
5 people are also afraid of heights,
and there are terrors on the road,
and the almond tree blossoms,
and the grasshopper is dragged along,
and the caper bush becomes useless;
for man goes to his eternal abode,
with mourners circling in the market-street –
6 before the silver cord is severed,
and the golden bowl is crushed,
and the jar is shattered at the spring,
and the pulley is smashed into the cistern,
7 and the dust returns to the earth as it was,
and the spirit returns to God, Who bestowed it.

In one of antiquity's most magnificent poems, Kohelet moves radically into symbolism, metaphor, and/or allegory. There have been many approaches to interpreting these phrases and symbols, with varied emphases on deterioration of bodily organs (grinders as teeth, those who see through the windows as eyes, guards as a variety of suggested strong muscles or limbs, etc.); a storm; the fall of night; or the abandonment (and/or disintegration) of a town or of an estate. Interspersed are direct descriptions of physical aging, approaching

a. In the feminine, possibly implying women (or, as a corporeal allegory, teeth).
b. Same term as "sound" earlier in the verse – can mean "voice."
c. "Singers" indicates women or birds.
d. Either individuals bent over or sound reduced.

death, and a funeral. By way of example, 12:2 is variously taken as reflections of the face, the approach of a storm, the inability to see well, or a changing series of symbols. As with much great poetry, it is counterproductive to reduce all to a single thread of meaning, and there is no indication that the poet sought one consistent set of symbols or an overriding allegory. (This eclectic approach follows many commentators.[34]) Nor should one stretch to find a logical ordering of sun, light, moon, stars – the poetry is more powerful without such technical manipulations. There is much multivalence, within which the poem speaks for itself.

That said, there does seem to be a vague structure to the description by stages. One is to remember the Creator "before…" (literally "up to the time when"), that preposition ("before") repeated three times (vv. 1, 2, and 6), creating stanzas. The first stanza would seem to speak of old age (or to be more precise, terminal illness whenever it arrives), the last stanza of death, with the middle stanza bridging the two (and therefore best read as applying to both, with possible reflections of a funeral and/or mourning). Thus, in this last section, Kohelet expands the implication of the dark horizon – from death to include the deterioration that precedes it.

Note the opening apocalyptic tone of 12:2, the sun darkening and the clouds returning right after a rain. The dimming of the sun is also clearly an indication of an end to life: in the book as a whole, "under the sun" indicates the land of the living, "not ever seeing the sun" refers to the stillborn (6:5), those who "see the sun" who are alive (7:11). The image of the sun's dimming is especially powerful in light of the earlier praise of being able to see it (11:7) and the permanence attributed to it at the beginning of the book (1:5). This final mention of the sun being so personalized (the "dimming" having to do with man, the beholder, not the sun), seems to confirm Kohelet's overall emphasis in the second half of the book on individual experience.

Verse 5 is particularly difficult. Some suggest that the almond tree blossoming may refer to the tips of the flowers turning white (about a month after blooming), symbolizing aging. The dragged grasshopper is variously associated with the burden of even the lightest load, stiff joints, or impotence (as interpreted by Rashi and others, in light of what follows). The caper bush was a reputed aphrodisiac. Some, on the other hand, deny the symbolic import of the images in this verse and suggest that they describe nature as a countermovement of rebirth just at the time of death (thus, NJPS translates as caper bush may "bud again," and "grasshopper" is emended to a kind of bush that regenerates).

Verse 6 should not be stretched into a single, consistent picture. Some find two metaphors – a broken lamp and an abandoned well – but the gold and silver are not necessarily to be taken literally. The strong poetic picture also hints at a funerary practice of breaking a pitcher and leaving the shards with the dead.[35]

Verse 7 clearly reflects Genesis 2:7 and 3:19 ("dust to dust"), and is in some conflict with Ecclesiastes 3:18–21 (including "Who knows if a man's spirit rises up while an animal's spirit sinks down to the earth?"). It does, however, correspond to Kohelet's newfound preference for life (see 9:4, with commentary). Kohelet, approaching death, does not say what he once said as a young man. Even if this verse does not quite affirm the relatively new belief in his time of a personalized afterlife, it minimally reflects the general biblical understanding that one's body houses something from God that survives death in some fashion.

The possible range of reader reactions to Kohelet's reversal extends all the way from seeing it as a sad reflection of human weakness on approaching death to a joyous celebration of final enlightenment, the wisdom that comes with age. One should nevertheless recall that Kohelet chillingly returns the body to the earth, the very "earth" that at the beginning of the book (v. 1:4) never changes, generation to generation.

In any case, verse 7 does not represent a retraction of all that he has said to that point, or even of large parts of it. It is, rather, a brief reflection on the world "above the sun," not the field of his inquiry. One nevertheless must add this to the general progression of the book, as Kohelet moves from preferring death to preferring life, from avoiding women to advising marriage, shifting his emphasis from observation to advice, and so on.

There are two other possible (not certain) reflections of his changes in attitude. One is that as he turns more and more at the end to others, rather than to himself, the dominance of the first-person singular ("I") almost disappears.[36] Second, in retrospect, if the fourth word in 12:1 is to be translated as "Creator" (see above), it would be his first use of that root, which is the less common biblical term for "create" but the one that opens Genesis 1. In light of his reservations about that Creation story (see the commentary on 1:3–11), this usage, too, could hint at renewed appreciation of his inherited tradition. His final thoughts (12:1–7), one notes, begin and end with God. Kohelet, who said at the start of his work that "there is nothing new under the sun" (1:9), has changed.

The final "spirit" is the same Hebrew word as "wind" in 1:6, which there goes round and round and here finally returns to God, an appropriate end to Kohelet's words (parallel to the body returning to earth, as noted above).

Death having spoken, nothing remains for Kohelet to say. The drama of the ending is brutally stark. One recalls that the first two poems (1:4–7 and 3:1–8) were each followed by long sections. Here the third poem would thus be expected to be an opening, but it is followed by nothing – literarily, an uncompromising declaration that death leaves no individuated continuation.

The Narrator, Looking Back

An Epilogue (12:8–14)

Reprise and Closure
Theme

יב:ח הֲבֵל הֲבָלִים אָמַר הַקּוֹהֶלֶת הַכֹּל הָבֶל׃

12:8 "Vapor of vapors," said Kohelet, "everything is vapor!"[a]

The restated theme is spoken by the narrator, as was the slightly longer version in the opening. It identifies Kohelet's major argument and also indicates that this narrator, whom we will now come to know, is himself linguistically skilled. (See the commentary on 1:2.) Only now will the narrator clarify his distance from the book, talking about Kohelet and providing a critique.

This enclosure, "vapor of vapors," would seem to imply a consistency. However, change did take place. There are two possible views, then, of the "errant" summary. Either the narrator is pictured as not being sensitive to the change or the repetition is somewhat ironic (and note that it is slightly less insistent, with three repetitions of "vapor," than the opening parallel in 1:2, with its five repetitions).

a. Echoing 1:2. See the note and commentary there, including the comments on the translation.

Final Narration
The Epilogue

יב:ט וְיֹתֵר שֶׁהָיָה קֹהֶלֶת חָכָם עוֹד לִמַּד־דַּעַת אֶת־הָעָם וְאִזֵּן וְחִקֵּר תִּקֵּן מְשָׁלִים הַרְבֵּה: י בִּקֵּשׁ קֹהֶלֶת לִמְצֹא דִּבְרֵי־חֵפֶץ וְכָתוּב יֹשֶׁר דִּבְרֵי אֱמֶת: יא דִּבְרֵי חֲכָמִים כַּדָּרְבֹנוֹת וּכְמַשְׂמְרוֹת נְטוּעִים בַּעֲלֵי אֲסֻפּוֹת נִתְּנוּ מֵרֹעֶה אֶחָד: יב וְיֹתֵר מֵהֵמָּה בְּנִי הִזָּהֵר עֲשׂוֹת סְפָרִים הַרְבֵּה אֵין קֵץ וְלַהַג הַרְבֵּה יְגִעַת בָּשָׂר: יג סוֹף דָּבָר הַכֹּל נִשְׁמָע אֶת־הָאֱלֹהִים יְרָא וְאֶת־מִצְוֹתָיו שְׁמוֹר כִּי־זֶה כָּל־הָאָדָם: יד כִּי אֶת־כָּל־מַעֲשֶׂה הָאֱלֹהִים יָבִא בְמִשְׁפָּט עַל כָּל־נֶעְלָם אִם־טוֹב וְאִם־רָע:

12:9 And moreover: Kohelet being a man of wisdom, he constantly taught knowledge to the people; weighing and investigating, he fixed[a] many maxims. **10** Kohelet sought to find <u>desirable</u> words while accurately recording[37] tr<u>uthful words</u>. **11** The words of the wise are like goads, and like embedded nails[b] are [the words of] the masters of the anthologies. They were given by one Shepherd.

12 And moreover: about them, my son, be admonished! The making[38] of many books has no end, and much study is a wearying of the flesh.

13 The final word: everything has been heard.[39] Fear <u>God and abide</u> <u>by His commands</u>! For this is all any man is, **14** for God will call every deed to judgment, including the hidden, be it good or bad.

The phrase "given by one Shepherd" is complex and dynamic. On an explanatory level, the reference is to the nails that were set by "a" shepherd (lower

a. Literally, "set straight," an enclosure to the book – see 1:15.
b. Goads were pointed shafts, but the verse seems to imply that nails embedded at the ends of shafts were also used to move cattle.

case). Were this the only meaning, however, "given by one shepherd" would follow "nails" or "goads." As placed, with the unnecessary emphasis on "one," there is also use of the known metaphor of God as a shepherd.[40] The phrase thus claims that these words of wisdom come from God. This is no minor claim, for in the Bible in general, Wisdom literature is considered a human product. The narrator's devotion to the genre may help explain his appreciation of Kohelet.

In this final selection,[a] then, the author of Ecclesiastes boldly provides an alternative voice to Kohelet, namely, a narrator (henceforth, in this section, the "epilogist"), who presents and ends the book (1:1–2; 7:27; and this section). Who is he? In concluding the book, he expresses his general appreciation of collected wisdom (12:11), indicating (in conjunction with the direct statement of vv. 9 and 10) his admiration for Kohelet, even if (as implied by the metaphor of the cattle goads and nails used to move oxen) there is a degree of pain involved. However, his subsequent words suggest serious reservations. He cautions against returning to Kohelet's search (v. 12), commending instead a traditional pattern of obedience.[41] He also asks the reader to "hear" (with its overtone of obedience), whereas Kohelet constantly urged the reader to "see" (with its overtone of questioning). Ironically, as he concludes his reflections on the book in this epilogue, he dismisses the unique value of any book.

It is fascinating that the epilogist in verses 13 and 14 does to Kohelet's words exactly what the latter did to words of earlier texts, which he took out of context and gave new implication. (For example, 3:14; 4:17; 5:3ff.; 5:6 – see the commentary on these verses.) So, too, the epilogist takes "everything," "fear God," "abide by command," "judgment," and "good" and reapplies them: "everything," which often means all of existence for Kohelet, now means all of Kohelet's words; "fear God," which Kohelet takes as wariness of a capricious God (5:6), returns to its biblical implication of religiosity; "abide by command," which implies prudence for Kohelet (8:5), returns to its original implication of devout obedience; "judgment" returns to its former implication of equitableness from Kohelet's institutional corruption (3:16) or inescapable destiny and doom (8:5, 6); and "good" regains its moral implication as opposed to Kohelet's use, "beneficial."

a. On the unity of the book and the epilogue, see Review Essays 3.1B, specifically, the excursus on excising the voice of the narrator from Ecclesiastes.

Although commending traditional stances, the epilogist's views nevertheless still reflect his admiration of Kohelet. One notes that he uses Kohelet's
terminology:[a] fear God (5:6), any man (5:18), abide by commands (8:5),
admonish (4:13), hearing/obedience (4:17), judgment (3:17), call to judgment
(11:9), no end (4:8, 16), plus wisdom, knowledge, word, weary, everything,
good, bad, and deed (several precedents each). He claims that Kohelet did
fix maxims (even though Kohelet said that one cannot "fix" God's twisted
things – 1:15). At the same time, his use of new terminology, including some
terms drawn from classic Wisdom literature [such as his address to "my son"
(v. 12), a convention of that literature,[b]] befits another voice.

The traditional epilogist describes Kohelet positively, and one now recalls
that it was this narrator who took care (1:1) to emphasize that Kohelet
descended from David, certainly one of the great figures in biblical history.
This appreciation from a traditionalist reminds the reader that Kohelet's frustrations had more to do with his failure to achieve harmony between observed
truth (i.e., empirical knowledge) and traditional beliefs (3:11 – "without man
ever finding out the deed[s] God has done, from beginning to end") than
with any thought of totally rejecting those beliefs. Kohelet discovered that
this world cannot confirm those beliefs and suggests how one can live with
that. That is different from abandoning those tenets. Even if Kohelet cannot
verify them, he does not deny them (even if at times his reinterpretations
are radical). Furthermore, by giving summary advice Kohelet implies that
his book was designed to help others to avoid going through the search he
pursued, and with it, experiencing the frustration of that search's ultimate
failure. He comes to "reveal" reality to the reader and to suggest how to get
along, not to propose continued search. All this seems to be enough to allow
the epilogist to present Kohelet's stance with admiration.

In any case, in terms of Ecclesiastes, the intricacy and tensions of Kohelet's
messages are now further complicated by the fact that the narrator also
expresses reservations. The reader, already challenged by the different voices
of Kohelet, his inner conflicts, and his shifts, now confronts the voice of an
enthusiast with other hesitations. This epilogist was himself challenged by
Kohelet and, having found his own way to appreciate him critically, seeks

a. See previous paragraph and Review Essays 3.1B.
b. For example, Proverbs 1:8 and 2:1.

to share Kohelet's words with the reader, adding emphatically that no more consideration is required.

Not so the author of Ecclesiastes, who created both Kohelet and the narrator/epilogist! In presenting all of Ecclesiastes, the <u>author</u> evidently sought to challenge his readers and to leave them with <u>more questions</u> than an<u>swers</u>, questions to which he hoped they would return repeatedly. In giving so much advice (note the irony of Kohelet's advice in 11:10, "Banish vexation from your heart"), Kohelet partially echoes the epilogist's "much studying is a wearying of the flesh." It is a prodigious achievement that the author's two characters, both Kohelet and the epilogist, end by recommending less future exploration and questioning, whereas he, the author, achieves the opposite effect. Any reader finishing Ecclesiastes is left with the whole narrative, and the questions live on.

In some Jewish communities, Ecclesiastes is read annually on Sukkot (the holiday of Tabernacles), becoming an insistent reminder of the <u>fragility</u> of <u>solutions</u>. By critically relating the story of Kohelet, who found no empirical evidence of God's workings "under the sun" and yet continued to speak within his community, Ecclesiastes is an invitation to dialogue and thought.

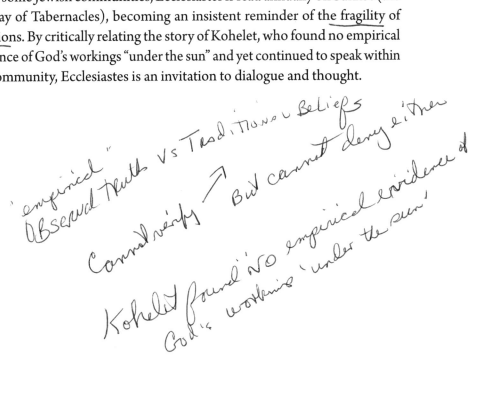

Review Essays and Further Thoughts

It is best to read the following consecutively. However, a reader interested in a particular section might proceed to it directly. Given that possibility, I sometimes repeat contentions and summaries, for which I apologize to the consecutive reader.

In the following pages I summarize and expand upon points included in the introduction and in the commentary and offer new perspectives. The essays are intended for all readers, not just researchers, so they do not include point-by-point rebuttals of alternative positions. When deemed appropriate, these are included in the endnotes.

I first discuss issues of content and context, emphasizing those areas wherein this commentary differs from others. Further on in these essays I deal with issues concerning the processes of translation and presentation.

1. The Content and Meaning of Ecclesiastes

Is there such a thing as *the* meaning of Ecclesiastes? Some modern literary approaches reject the very idea that a text has a defined range of implications and locate all meaning and significance with the readers in whatever way they may interpret it.[42] However, the present commentary adopts a different position, namely that the original text does make certain statements, limiting the range of authentic interpretations. I proceed, then, to explore the meaning of the text.

Two reservations concerning other interpretations and approaches are immediately in order. The first is that Ecclesiastes is not a text in philosophy. Thinking otherwise, interpreters have offered a range of mutually exclusive explanations of the book's principal and principled positions. All of these interpretations err in overreaching, that is, in trying to impose a philosophical presentation on a work of imagination. They also err by omission in not giving due attention to development within the book.

The second reservation is that despite commentators who seek consistent and/or one- (or even two-) dimensional descriptions, this wonderful tale is a reflection of life's intricacy. Complexity is not a fault, but a virtue. Many times ambiguity, multivalence, vagueness, and uncertainty are valued parts of a text. A great literary character is much larger than any narrow description, and certainly in the case of Ecclesiastes, reductionism does not befit either this work or its lead persona.

1.1. Elements That Cannot Be Ignored

The following elements may be seen as the grid upon which any description of proposed meaning stands. To ignore them is to misrepresent the book. Ecclesiastes is a work of imagination, as any ancient reader would have appreciated. There was no king named Kohelet, nor did any king in antiquity "resign" to become a teacher/preacher. (The story as told after chapter 2 reflects a non-king as speaker.[43])

The framework of Kohelet's search in the book is what is "under the sun," a term used often, which does not quite indicate all of reality. In biblical cosmology, the world is divided by the "firmament," where God placed the heavens and within them the sun. God is sometimes located in the heavens, or above them (including by Kohelet, 5:1). "Under the sun" indicates all of reality *knowable to man by direct experience*. As Longman writes, "In the Bible this viewpoint is unique to Qohelet."[44]

Kohelet resorts to empirical evidence (i.e., evidence dependent exclusively on experience and observation), he being the primary source of his analysis (though inherited traditions are cited). He combines personal experience (in his words, an "experiment") and observation of others, primarily in separate units (parts I and II, respectively). He seeks to verify what is beneficial to man (using two terms, "beneficial" and "advantage"), the "candidates" for worthwhile pursuits being drawn from his religious tradition (such as righteousness and its implied reward), the commitments found in Wisdom literature (ranging from common sense to gaining wisdom itself, hard work, planning, and so on), to well-known goals of society (wealth, power, position, enjoyment).

In light of his efforts, Kohelet shares his insights and suggestions for how best to act (and not to act) and what pursuits to choose. He also offers attitudinal suggestions. His repeated advice is to seize upon enjoyment when one is given the opportunity. There are two speakers in Ecclesiastes: the narrator, who speaks briefly (1:1–2; 7:27b; 12:8–14), and Kohelet (all other texts). There is a degree of disagreement between them.

All this relates to the book as a narrative, its essential description. Nevertheless, even though the book presents no single ordered approach to life or to its understanding, one can see that the character Kohelet comes to some basic conclusions about the world. These are, in fact, a matter of fairly widespread consensus among commentators, which according to Fox, can be summarized:

BA si Con clusis about the world

1. Everything in this life is, in some way, inadequate –worthless, vain, futile, transient, or senseless, and injustices abound.

2. There is no point in striving too hard for anything, whether wealth or wisdom.

3. It is best simply to enjoy what you have when you have it and to fear God.[45]

Again, however, Kohelet is a character, and Ecclesiastes is the book. The book proposes that one confront Kohelet in all his complexity, which is very different from "the book wants you to think like Kohelet." Therefore, the three statements listed immediately above are only a starting point in reading Ecclesiastes, not its conclusion, and, further, there are subtle developments related to them. Finally, and quite obviously, no great work of literature can be summarized by any three points.

To restate the overview in brief: *This narrative is a literary tale of a man who sought – through experience, observation, and analysis of this world – to test and hopefully to verify the values for, and truths about, life, as propagated by his religious tradition, the tradition of Wisdom literature, and pursuits held dear by society in general. It is also the tale of his basic failure to achieve that, his reactions to that failure, and his advice on how to live in a world where such verification is unavailable. It is a tale told retrospectively, a summary of experiences and thoughts. All is presented as a first-person report framed within the words of a countervoice, a narrator with reservations about the very text he narrates.*

1.2. *Understanding the Character Kohelet*

Great literature lives on in the interpretation of the motivations, characteristics, and descriptions of major figures: the greater the literature, the closer to life; and the closer to life, the more difficult it is to offer a definitive analysis. To a degree, then, "understanding" the person Kohelet is an eternally renewed challenge. That said, there are parameters that should be taken into account, over and above the totality of his observations, deeds, and advice, as recorded.

The clearest information can be drawn from the epilogue, which, while reflecting a specific view of Kohelet (by the narrator), would seem to contain a basic outline of Kohelet's endeavor and the categories to which one would assign him. In the epilogue, Kohelet is seen as a master of wisdom, heir and transformer of tradition, a teacher, and a seeker of truth. Beyond that, the range of the book further indicates that he reached an old age, that he evidently consistently pursued his quest, and, by the time of the final "publication" of the book by the narrator, had died. The range of types of literature attributed to him would indicate an individual who was very learned, skilled, and creative. The three major poems (1:4–8; 3:1–8; and 12:1–7) are particularly magnificent, and the use of the opening pseudo-autobiography as king in Jerusalem is daring and, as far as I know, strikingly different.

The opening story of the experience of a king (chapters 1 and 2) is a fiction within a fiction, the character of Kohelet adopting thereby a technique that authors used in antiquity: attributing a work to a great earlier figure.[46] In Ecclesiastes, the imagined story is indeed creative – a tale of an incredibly rich and wise king (the model of whom must be Solomon), and who better to test the advantages of wisdom, wealth, and enjoyment? However, this "king" (unthinkably, in antiquity) evolves away from that role and, for the rest of the book, functions as an observer, analyst, and advisor (thus giving him access to a wide range of other peoples' experiences that would not have come under the purview of a king).

One of the questions in tracing the character of Kohelet is to what degree that pseudo-autobiography is reflective of Kohelet himself. This king experiences much "vexation" and "pain." He indicates that he "hates" both life and his material goods, and he sees himself as being in "despair." Clearly this king is determined to learn through experience. If this account reflects the character Kohelet, there is an unhappy pall over his life, ranging somewhere from melancholy to misery. In a general manner of speaking, part II supports those descriptions of Kohelet as culled from part I and hints by use of language echoing those two first chapters that Kohelet shares many qualities with the king.

Most of the rest of the book is based on Kohelet's observations, usually of experiences not his own. Thus, when he speaks of the great anger one has in leaving this world with nothing, just as one entered it, it is attributed to his observation of others, and the "anger" cannot definitively be ascribed to Kohelet himself. However, in verse 7:15 he does label his own life "vaporous." His exhaustion, deriving from his total dedication to his search, as reflected in 8:16, seems honest. Further, when he speaks of the impossibility of human beings gaining true understanding (e.g., 7:23ff.), he would seem to acknowledge his own failure, for that was the essence of his quest.

Many interpreters have concluded reasonably that the repeated expression of concern for not having an heir or not knowing who would control an inheritance reflects an absence of children (only at one point does the text in part II break through with a first-person plaint, in 4:8, and it precisely bemoans the lack of an heir). Further, the section denigrating women (7:26–29) seems to hint at an unhappy history in this regard and at the probability that he was not married (or if once married, is no longer so).[47]

How did Kohelet feel about God? To a degree, of course, one could say that since God is the Creator, everything in the book is about how Kohelet views God. However, Kohelet's chosen arena is "under the sun," that is, in the experience of life. Does he go beyond that and speak of God or give hints of his relationship to Him?

In truth, most statements about God have to do with evidence of Him and His doings on earth. Some are clearly drawn from tradition – God is the Creator, He is to be feared, He is found in heaven, He is powerful, He is demanding, He does (or will) disburse justice, He is not subject to questioning by humans, and so on – although subtleties and contexts differentiate many of these from similar biblical statements. Any presumed reactions by Kohelet are only a matter of speculation.

That said, there are some verses that seem to imply reservations on Kohelet's part. When God is said to "give" man things that are a "bad concern" (1:13), it is hard to deny a tone of criticism. "Who can fix what He has twisted?" (7:13) is certainly a critique, as would be any situation where God is named directly as He Who entices and then denies (e.g., giving wealth but preventing its enjoyment, 6:2; giving man a desire for knowledge that cannot be attained, 3:10–11). These, then, express reservations, but where they are placed on a scale of reactions, from puzzlement or questioning on one end to resentment or anger on the other, is moot, and the judgment must be left to the reader.

1.3. First-Person Speech and Its Effects

Kohelet's views are presented primarily in his own words, as first-person speech. As Bickerman summarized, "For the first time in Jewish sapiential literature the Sage gives preference to his 'I'. . . . Again and again Kohelet stresses his personal experience of life."[48] In a general manner of speaking, arguments presented as first-person experiences and conclusions are inherently less convincing than a third-person "objective" presentation. Even if logically a claim of truth presented as "fact" in the third person relies on the speaker as much as the same claim framed as first-person speech ("I saw…I concluded… I say…"), the latter seems less objective.

Therefore, the reader is moved not only to weigh Kohelet's stances, but also his character: his (perhaps errant) assumptions, his subjectivity owing to time and circumstance, arguments he did not (or could not) know or consider,[49] and even character flaws that may have influenced his judgment. As in so many encounters with great literary figures, the reader is invited into a complex relationship with the character and his words.[50]

This is far from how one would present a philosophy, since as a rhetorical tactic, a first-person presentation undermines the very credibility of statements. However, as Ecclesiastes is a narrative, not a treatise, the use of the first person is most appropriate. One should also note that in the course of his life Kohelet came to doubt anyone's ability – including his own – to understand fully what he or she observed (e.g., 3:11; 8:17). His words, then, challenge his own presentation.[a]

1.4. *Enjoyment* vs haggiveess

The primary structure of Ecclesiastes is, as amazing as it may seem, built around "enjoyment." This term is the prime marker that delimits most sections and is the repeated refrain of the book.[b] This enjoyment, when it arrives, is seen as a "gift," a free-will beneficence from God (see 5:18), unrelated to reward. Rather, it is an opportunity, and Kohelet's message is not to miss it.[c]

Nevertheless, one should pause to question the nature of this consistent advice. It seems to indicate (almost counterintuitively) that Kohelet did experience (or at least seek) some degree of happiness. However, it is vital to distinguish between "enjoyment" (*simchah*) as recommended by Kohelet and "happiness," as we might illustrate it through a recurring term in Psalms, *ashrei* (as found by way of example in the opening of Psalms, "*Happy* is the man

---

a. See section 1.5C below.

b. The term "joy/enjoy" (*s-m-ch*) appears in 2:1, 2, 10, 26; 3:12, 22; 4:16; 5:18; 7:4; 8:15; 9:7; 10:19; and 11:8, 9. Its synonym, "experience good" appears in 2:1 and 7:14 (see commentaries there). See section 5 below.

c. See section 1.5C below for a more detailed description.

who has not walked in the counsel of the wicked"). *Ashrei* indicates a deep sense of satisfaction, calm, and completion.[51] Not so Kohelet's enjoyment! It cannot be divorced from its context, where it is an exceptional opportunity, not a quality of life. One can imagine Kohelet being fully involved in joyous moments but not living a "happy" life. His is a sober and somber existence, and his appreciation of bits of enjoyment emerge in no small part from his recognition of their exceptional nature.[a] His attitude toward laughter is negative (2:2 – and in 7:3, it is worse than the otherwise uniformly bad "vexation"), but he does, at the end, opt for a "good heart" (approximately "cheer," the result of feasting and drinking).

One implication of the recommended enjoyment (and of his other words of advice) is that Kohelet cares. He is ultimately a teacher who wishes to communicate what he considers vital. "The enjoyment theme…has a… great…role as an intimate address to the reader… [It] engenders a feeling of caring and openness…. This effect builds a sense of trust…. He is an honest and empathetic soul."[52]

1.5. Change within Ecclesiastes

The most ironic and unexpected discovery in Ecclesiastes is that there *is* something new under the sun. Set against Kohelet's observations of an un-understandable, unchangeable world is the man himself, who ever so subtly grows and develops. It is he who changes; he is not at the end of the book who he was at the beginning. It is that progress that the reader confronts through careful reading.

The book's focus moves radically. Part I is set on a maximal stage, two poems describing the broadest possible movements of nature and time, these surrounding the hyperbolic story of the richest and wisest man on earth. Part II focuses on others, to include both broad observations and anecdotal incidents. It is in part II that one begins to encounter Kohelet's empathy with others. Part III narrows down further, toward the quiet of dying and death. The contrast between the dynamic and ever-challenging Kohelet and the narrator, whose dry comments beginning and end pale in comparison, adds further dynamism to the text.

a. Kohelet does progress from simply observing the advantages of joy to advising one to seek it and to advising cheer through eating and drinking – see section 1.5C.

These developments open the reader to the possibility of others throughout the work, with close attention paid to "contradictions," lest some of them prove to be changes that occur as the book progresses. That progress is accompanied by literary markers. On close reading, one discovers: (a) terms that change their primary connotations as they reappear; (b) terms that cease (or begin) appearing; and (c) shifts in concentration, all of which I detail below.

The import of this pattern of development cannot be overstated. It bolsters the understanding of Ecclesiastes as a narrative, confirming both a time sequence and a plot of sorts, a tracing of the impact of his experiences on Kohelet. True, there is no consecutive story timeline. Nevertheless the changes reflect progression and occur in a comprehensible cumulative pattern in the text, parallel to Kohelet's aging.

I now cite details and evidence of the changes, to be followed by a personal interpretation.

1.5A. LITERARY MARKERS OF CHANGE – TERMS THAT ARISE AND FALL

- ANGUISH. One of the most repeated words in the first half of the book, this term does not appear after 6:9.

- VAPOR. This is a central term throughout the work, but apart from the framing summaries spoken by the narrator (1:2; 12:9), it appears much less often in the second half of the book;[53] moreover, within that second half, it becomes personalized, often describing an individual life ("his…, your…, my life of vapor") and is much less likely to appear as a summary.[a]

- "I" REMOVAL. No other biblical work so concentrates on the speaker and his views. It is thus striking that the first person disappears from the end of Kohelet's words, the last usage being in 10:7 (apart from 12:1, where the first person does not refer to Kohelet), a final echo after a gradually diminishing use.

- CREATOR. In light of the examples in these paragraphs (on change), it is possible (though not certain) that another development is reflected in Kohelet's use of "Creator" in 12:1, an affirmation of the Genesis account of Creation as opposed to his earlier reservations.[b]

a. See section 4.1B for further comment.
b. See commentary on part I, section 1 and on verse 12:1.

1.5B. LITERARY MARKERS OF CHANGE – SHIFTS IN EMPHASIS

- DEATH. Mortality hangs like a cloud over most of Ecclesiastes, often articulated indirectly (such as through the use of the term "destiny," thoughts
on the identity of heirs, concern over being forgotten, and so on). There
is at the same time an ever-growing focus on death as a personal concern.
Clusters of particular concentration are 3:19–21; 6:4–6, 11–12; and 8:8; with
great emphasis in part II, section 5 (9:1–6); and culminating in the poem
of old age and death, 12:1–7.

- HEART. The heart is the center of thought and affect throughout the Bible.
There is a shift in the areas of the heart's concern within the book.[54] Only
toward the end does the "heart" move from focusing on learning, declaring,
searching, and so on, to enjoyment (9:7; 11:9–10).

- WHAT ADVANTAGE? The question of "what advantage" fades into disuse
after 6:11.[55] There may also be import to a concentration on "who" questions thereafter, possibly befitting the growing concern some commentators find with the "formation of the individual" over "broader intellectual
questions."[56]

- ADVICE. Kohelet moves toward and into advice by stages, at first only in
terms of the initial observations of the advantage of enjoyment (2:26; 3:12),
and then with "better" activities (third-person observations, especially in
chapter 4), finally moving on to direct bidding. Further, Kohelet begins
to address his readers as "you" only from 4:17, where he also begins to use
imperatives. There is a growing proportion of advice vis-à-vis observation
as the book progresses.

- SUN. The sun evolves by stages, schematically: (a) one of the unchanging
cyclical elements that demonstrate that man can gain no advantage; (b) the
limitations of the book's inquiry ("under the sun"); (c) a personal source
of pleasure (11:7); and (d) in darkening, a symbol of approaching death, as
its import moves from its essence to its reality in the eye of the beholder.
It thus undergoes a process of personalization not unlike "vapor" (above).

- METAPHOR AND SIMILE. Apart from the term "vapor," there is only limited use of metaphor or simile until chapter 7.[57] This tendency increases
from that point on, and the final poem is a virtual flood of metaphors.

- END POINTS. Not a change, but a possible hint at progression is the opening of the book with its emphasis on the world and the end of the book with its emphasis on death.

1.5C. "CONTRADICTIONS," BETTER EXPLAINED AS CHANGE (LISTED IN THE ORDER OF THE APPEARANCE OF THE CHANGE)

- ENJOYMENT. This value appears to evolve radically. When Kohelet first encounters it, he finds no inherent value therein (2:1, 2), but by the end of the pseudo-autobiography, he finds it the best one can hope for, and thereafter holds on to that position. His first references to enjoyment emphasize that it comes upon one unexpectedly, a gift from God, of which one should take advantage (as in 7:14). As he approaches the end, he specifically uses the imperative to tell the young to enjoy (11:9), and he recommends enjoyment to his heart (see "heart" entry above). This area of change is bolstered by the development of "good heart" (below), emphasizing cheer in feasting and drinking.

- HIS ABILITY TO UNDERSTAND. The basis of the king's grand experiment is his ability to learn and analyze, but even as he proceeds through the pseudo- autobiography, he reflects that the assumption itself may be wrong, the clearest articulation of which comes in 7:23ff. – no one can understand.

- GOOD HEART. This is a type of joy associated with eating and drinking (Prov. 15:15; Esther 1:7; 5:9), approximately, "cheer." Kohelet astonishingly first suggests pursuit of a "good heart" through anger and vexation (7:3), but later shifts back to the accepted suggestion of drinking (9:7; 11:9).

- LIFE. Kohelet's negative experiences lead him to express a preference for death over life (4:2) and then even a higher estimation of the stillborn over some of the living (6:3). He later switches radically to a preference for life (9:4).

- WOMEN. Kohelet moves beyond his negative view of women (7:26–29) to advice to seek out a loving wife (9:9).

- THE SPIRIT OF MAN. In Kohelet's last statement, he recalls the ascension of the spirit (life force) back to God,[a] about which he had earlier expressed doubt (3:21).

a. Even though this is not an individuated afterlife (see the commentary).

- REWARD AND PUNISHMENT. Less certainly, Kohelet may reflect change back to greater acceptance of some overall plan of reward and punishment.[58]

1.5D. THE EARLIEST INDICATION OF CHANGE – THE FIRST TWO POEMS

In 1:4–7 and 3:1–8, Kohelet records two poems, written in a two styles far removed from the rest of the book. Read out of context, both poems are beautifully ambiguous, with a range of meanings that might be seen as depressing or encouraging. In context, however, both are given a narrower and negative interpretation ("What advantage can man have?").[a] Thus change is reflected even at the beginning of the book, as Kohelet seems to have cited his own earlier poems, narrowing their scope in light of experience.

1.5E. THE IRONY OF IRONIES: IS THERE NOTHING NEW UNDER THE SUN?

Sometimes a striking phrase or verse gains undue centrality. Only once does Kohelet say, "There is nothing new under the sun."[b] Ecclesiastes testifies to the opposite, but on the personal rather than the universal level. The fallacy was in the application of rules of the natural world to the realm of the living. It is he, Kohelet, who changes, in real if sometimes subtle ways. It is probably his awareness that people grow that underlies his turning to advice and teaching.

1.5F. ONE POSSIBLE SUMMARY OF CHANGE

Any analysis of these changes is much less certain than is their appearance. That said, I suggest the following as a personal reading, not to close off other options, but to encourage them. Other readings can be equally valid.

The strong emphasis on death at the end, the disappearance of "anguish," and the disappearance of "I" set a tone of finality and hint that the text, although not originally written sequentially, does reflect changes that come about with age, to the time of death. The tone of these changes is comprehensible and understandable, and can be described as more trustful of received

---

a. See the end of the comments on both poems in the commentary.
b. Verse 1:9, expanded in the next verse and restated in other terms in 3:15, both in reference to the first two poems, noted above.

traditions, more open to compromise, and less trusting of his prior observations and conclusions. Kohelet also becomes more sensitive to his role as a teacher (more advice, more use of metaphor, which is a classic technique for involving an audience, and less concern with himself).

One can also speak of a move away from philosophical musings toward personal urgency. If in the early parts of the work a reader feels a desire to debate with the speaker, at the end, that reader feels a desire to meet Kohelet and ease his pain.

None of the above notions (which, again, are offered only as possibilities) represents an *evaluation* of the progression. By way of example, one person could see his aging process here as a condemnable weakening of resolve, whereas another would see it as commendable newly achieved wisdom.

1.6. Answers and Questions: The Essence of Ecclesiastes

The single most frequent mistake commentators make is to overstate the nature of Ecclesiastes. One should not expect a tale of search to be a developed philosophy.[59] That would be a different volume.

In that regard, one should take note of some recent readings of Ecclesiastes that sense a movement toward a philosophical resolution as the text ends. One modern commentary suggests two broad stages in Kohelet's words: "tearing down" (subtitled the "subversion of meaning") and then "building up" (the "reconstruction of meaning," that is, "discovering ways of creating clarity and gratification in a confusing and indifferent world"[60]). This, in fact, is a widespread and popular understanding of the book. Another interpreter, adopting a similar approach, cites a three-stage "rhetorical strategy": ethos, destabilization, and restabilization.[61] Yet another commentary suggests that Kohelet replaces the model of seeking understanding or knowledge (which has failed) with one of seeking enjoyment out of life.[62]

These approaches show admirable appreciation of Kohelet's attempts to find a way to get along as best as one can in life. They certainly take account of contradictions within the text, although they do not suggest an awareness that the changes proceed by degrees as the text progresses. However, in proposing "resolution," they go too far. For one, they ignore the great concentration in the book on sections that "tear down" as opposed to those that "build up." Indeed, even the terms "build up" or "restabilization," which might apply to recommendations to seek some joy and be a little wise, hardly befit the oft-stated advice to proceed cautiously, which is almost a warning, "watch out, lest…" (e.g., 8:2–5, "keep the king's command…for he can do whatever he wishes"; 10:20).[63]

Is there, then, "reconstruction"? The truth, as so often in this book, is somewhat unclear. One must not discount words of advice from the character Kohelet, nor those from the narrator, but they are scarcely a "program." Further, contradictions remain in the world, and most of Kohelet's advice clearly hints at "the best that one can do."[64] Finally, recalling the narrative nature of the book, suggestions remain forever in the area of food for thought. There is no "reconstructed" view of life here.

More to the point is that the cumulative effect of Ecclesiastes's narrative may indicate change in Kohelet, but for the reader, the end certainly does not "overcome" the beginning in any way. No reader can leave Ecclesiastes without carrying away the weight and detail of the failed search. Moreover, no one reading the first-person narrative can accept Kohelet's conclusions as definitive, especially as he reverses himself in several ways. Whereas the character Kohelet may feel a sense of resolution (or better, "maximal accommodation") at the end, the reader does not.

This means that Ecclesiastes has a lot more to do with asking questions than supplying definitive answers. Undoubtedly there will be some who bridle at the suggestion that a book of the Bible seeks to challenge religious thinking rather than suggest a system of belief and action. However, that is exactly what this book does.[65] It joins other great works (the Book of Job and many psalms, such as Psalm 27, might serve as examples) in an ongoing commitment to open-eyed religious thinking. This is not a failure nor is it a reflection of religious thought that had not yet reached maturity.[66] Rather, it is one reflection of biblical religious thought, namely, its being firmly based in the context of the limits of human understanding.

The book, then, leads to a more focused but ultimately serious point. Ecclesiastes suggests that one's approach to life must be open-eyed. It must take account of the world that is knowable – that is, the world as Kohelet experienced it. Kohelet does have specific pieces of advice as to how to get along, and particularly that one should take advantage of enjoyment as much as possible, but he does not prescribe a detailed theology or pattern of thought. The wide range of meta-interpretations of Ecclesiastes in fact testifies to this, as the book's advice can be incorporated in a number of thought "systems." Ecclesiastes is not a prescription for all of one's life, but a demand for what one must *include* in one's thinking. It is a book that ends not with a "!" but with a "?!" It is not an answer to all challenges, but a challenge to all answers.

That Ecclesiastes has been seen as part of widely varied systems of thought and philosophy is a compliment to its still relevant contribution as a serious encounter with empirical knowledge. In the end, the failure to find clear evidence of how to act, combined with the determination to return to try again, is not a sign of the failure of the book, but of its success. It remains not a guide, but a goad. It does, however, provide enough of an anchor to encourage and support the further quest. In Kohelet's advice and in his conservative mode – not rebelling against the system, accepting God's dominance, implying that teaching and memory are themselves a comfort – the persona is, despite all, a reassurance to the reader. Ecclesiastes as a whole goes one step further, for the narrator, more traditionally oriented than Kohelet, finds the book worthwhile. Both Kohelet and the narrator thus seem to be exemplars of finding a way to live with questions.

1.7. Beyond That, the Reader

Finally it is worth noting that this book foreshadows many postmodern literary approaches, which grant so major a role to the reader in the interpretive process.[67] Ecclesiastes was written to offer that role to the reader! It is an invitation to dialogue and to thought,[68] as one commentator has put it, written "in order to provoke readers to the formation of their own judgment."[69]

Any other words of description belong properly to each reader, not to a commentator. Adjectives for the character Kohelet such as "obsessed," "intense," "tragic," "sad," "frustrated," "levelheaded," "courageous," and so on belong in that analysis, not in a commentary, as do summaries of one's relationship to the character – "awe," "pity," "admiration," "sympathy," etc. The degree to which Kohelet's positions undermine or in fact underpin tradition is also a matter of personal understanding.

It is, however, worthwhile to repeat my principal contention one more time. This is not a philosophical tract, but the tale of Kohelet's search. It is as a narrative that it has had and will continue to have influence on the religious, theological, and philosophical thought of its readers.

2. Three Contexts of Ecclesiastes: Bible, Literature, and Time

Ecclesiastes is often (subconsciously) viewed in light of its contexts, three of which tend to impose themselves on the thinking of interpreters: the Hebrew Bible, the classification of literature, and the time of writing. Each must be carefully explored for what it does and does not define. I comment on them in turn.

2.1. The Biblical Environment

2.1A. ECCLESIASTES'S PLACE IN THE BIBLE

Ecclesiastes is part of the third section of the Hebrew Bible, commonly titled "Writings" or in Latin, "Hagiographa." By the time of writing (see below), the Torah (Pentateuch, the first five books of the Bible) had already been canonized, and it is cited in Ecclesiastes and creatively interpreted. The opening of Ecclesiastes, "The words of...," is identical to that of Jeremiah and Amos, two prophets, possibly indicating that the second section of the Bible, Prophets, was at least in the proto-canonization stage, as is supported by other evidence.[70]

Most of the works in Writings differ from the earlier books of the Bible. They are neither prophecies nor the tales of prophets, and they do not claim divine inspiration. They neither legislate nor preach. Rather, they are literature – tales, musings, collections, and poetry – authors sharing their confrontations with the complexity of life.[71] The Hebrew Bible is more than what is implied by "Scripture," a term that might be taken to imply "sacred" by the modern ear. "Bible" means essentially "books," no more and no less, and the Writings, in particular, are best represented as good literature.

Ecclesiastes is one of the works dealing with the challenging interaction between religious tradition and experience. Other "similar" biblical works differ in their approaches. Job presents extended dialogues, testing explanations of suffering. Psalms presents poetic, individual explorations that are personal, intense, and varied. Ecclesiastes is yet a different model, a tale of a failed effort leading to advice, all meant to challenge the thinking of the reader.

2.1B. THE QUESTION OF CANONIZATION

Nevertheless, how did Ecclesiastes, built around Kohelet's negative conclusions, including the lack of evidence for God's justice in this world, and filled with contradictions, become part of the Bible? The path was not smooth, and we have early evidence of much soul searching. The Mishnah bears testimony to disagreement among the rabbis concerning Ecclesiastes's biblical status (*Yadaim* 3:5),[72] basically setting the School of Shammai (against canonization) against the School of Hillel (for canonization). The sources reflect an ultimate acceptance. Later, as recorded in the Talmud and parallel sources,[73] some rabbis sought to withdraw the book from public access, but a complex of considerations explain its inclusion.

First, we know little of the process of canonization, other than that the rabbis disagreed on which books were to be included, and the only later record we have (see the previous endnote) is one of a failed attempt to censor books already accepted, which applied to several texts. Despite the possible implication that the rabbis decided such matters, we know not how (or indeed "if"!), nor are we aware of all the considerations. Thus some opine that the primary factor in many cases was *not* an official imprimatur but an informal popular acceptance, an admittedly ill-defined general consensus. In that regard, one notes the appearance of Ecclesiastes among the Dead Sea Scrolls (parallel in time to early rabbinic sources) and the fact that an early Talmudic rabbi cites Ecclesiastes as one would a biblical quotation.[74] These facts support the assumption of early approval.

Second, for all Kohelet's questioning and doubt, he neither denies historical records nor contradicts prescribed patterns of behavior.

Third, emerging Judaism never had unity of practice or thought, and to the degree that there was any such effort, it had more to do with practice than thought.

Fourth, there is a wide range of inclusions in the Bible. The early Israelite society gave birth not just to a religion but to a civilization. As noted above, much of Writings is simply great literature, and by that qualification alone, Ecclesiastes surely merits inclusion. The location, the literary references, and the adopted relation to King David (1:1) are but the most obvious of the indications of Israel as the cultural home of this work.[75]

Fifth, the thought that Solomon wrote the book can be traced to a first mention in about 200 BCE,[76] and it could have helped authenticate the book in people's eyes.

Finally, even though the epilogue by the narrator was not created in order to make the book acceptable (see the commentary for this interpretive conclusion), the content thereof certainly could have enhanced that effect.[77] The Talmud attributes Ecclesiastes's non-withdrawal from circulation to the fact that it begins and ends with "standard Torah."[78]

Beyond that, Ecclesiastes finds a natural home in the biblical realm of conversation. The book moves within the world of biblical ethical monotheism, and to the degree that the narrative leaves a "message," it is one of issues to be carried forward as the presumed reader works out personal understandings and accommodations.

Further, the book would be considered undermining only to the extent that the Bible sought to present unequivocal answers in matters of faith, but much of the Bible is comfortable in leaving questions open and in providing a variety of answers, prescriptions, or narratives. Indeed, certain sections of the Bible, including Ecclesiastes as here interpreted, Job, and many psalms can be seen as demanding questioning, not just allowing for the same. The Bible even includes many conflicting versions of history and laws, not just matters of belief and understanding. A proper appreciation of this framework allows anyone, from religionist through secularist, to approach Ecclesiastes freely, a proffered exploration of life, not a religious norm.

2.2. The Literary Environment of Ecclesiastes

"Kohelet was a writer of striking originality."[79] That accurate observation should caution interpreters against easily pigeonholing this book as one type of literature or another. Indeed, the opening term, "The words of," recalls Jeremiah and Amos,[a] two books that are collections not only of different pieces

a. The term also appears at the start of Proverbs 30 and 31.

from different times but also different types of literature: prose and poetry, history and parable, description and metaphor, and dialogues and visions.

Terms are too easily proposed as an overview of Ecclesiastes – "essay," "autobiography," "narrative," "philosophy," and so on. All are partial truths. The complexity far outweighs any encompassing appellation. By way of example, Kohelet seems to cite three of his own poems, and then twice provides an interpretation, but clearly not the only original possible interpretation.[a] From the beginning of the work this complexity is clear, as one can see from the progression. The author opens with the words of a narrator, who introduces Kohelet, who soon presents a pseudo-autobiography of himself as a fictitious king! This unit gives way to another, a cyclical presentation of observations and advice. Recurrent claims, both about the world and about how to live, create a certain unity, but those claims exist in the midst of a narrative that exhibits elements of change and growth, and even contradictions.

Thus no one literary characterization (and these, one must recall, are drawn from modernity, not antiquity) would seem to be encompassing. Nevertheless, one term may be more appropriate than others. "Narrative" is probably the closest description, and one interpreter has written a full volume so proposing.[80] That term fits, but not quite exactly. It has been suggested that there are four features common to all narratives (events, plot, first-person narration, and motif), leading to the following definition: "the representation of real or fictive events or situations in a time sequence."[81] It is possible to argue that both the four elements and the definition hold for Ecclesiastes, but that argument would be difficult, and ultimately moot.[82] One certainly can accept those interpreters who have found "narrative elements," "narrative threads," "autobiographical elements," and so on in Ecclesiastes.[83] However, the book also includes Wisdom instruction, poetry, and analysis. It is, indeed, a unique piece of literature. I use "narrative," having expressed my reservations, as the best approximation, sometimes using "tale," but only for the sake of variety.

Other overviews might be acceptable, as long as the reader keeps in mind that all are inadequate. At the same time, it is vital to disqualify the overview that the book is the explication of a philosophy. I contend with others that many modern commentaries err in trying to apply philosophical categories to Ecclesiastes, which assumption necessarily includes a close scrutiny of

a. See section 1.5D.

internal consistency. This is not a philosophy nor is it a philosophical tract, and one should not expect insistently uniform thinking any more than one would expect to find it, by way of example, in any play (even if presented as a long monologue).

This is a work of imagination, revealing a fascinating persona and his struggles. The character's insights (and/or the reader's critiques thereof!) can impact on theology or philosophy, and were possibly meant to do so, but they should not be confused with either of them. This difference between philosophy and Ecclesiastes has been noted by others: "He offered no philosophy but simply opposed the experience of a skeptic to the orthodox system of morality."[84] Like much good literature, this book is reflective of a life and of living, and neither can be painted in monochrome.[85]

2.3. The Date of Ecclesiastes and Its International Environment

The long-standing tradition that Solomon, king of Israel (reign ca. 961–921 BCE), wrote Ecclesiastes is both too literal an understanding of the attribution to Kohelet "son of David"[a] and yet an accurate reflection of the speaker's first-tale imagery being *based on* Solomon, with his great wealth and wisdom (1 Kings 5:1–14). Kohelet does present himself as a king, one clearly *modeled* on Solomon. However, that theoretical dating bears no possible historical veracity. Interpreters have long recognized that the linguistics of this book reflect, approximately, the mid-third century BCE, toward the end of the biblical period. It also shows a strong Aramaic influence,[86] another indication of the relatively late date. The first section of the Bible, the Torah, had long been canonized (but not until after the First Temple period), and Kohelet cites and interprets sections in his own unique way.[b] The text, on the other hand, cannot postdate the Apocryphal book *The Wisdom of Sirach* (*Ecclesiasticus*), ca. 190 BCE, which reacts to Ecclesiastes.[87]

This dating raises the question of the familiarity of the author with Greek culture and specifically with intellectual movements of that time. Although there is no solid indication of Greek linguistic influence in the book (probably

a. The term is also used for three other sons of David (cf. II Sam. 13:1 and II Chron. 11:18.)
b. Verses 3:14; 4:17; 5:3ff.; 5:6; and 7:20. See the commentary.

thus locating the author in the Land of Israel, as opposed to Egypt, where Greek was sometimes spoken), connection to these schools of thought is often proposed, at least by way of initial exploration.

Even an overview of the many detailed studies of connections to Greek thought would be far beyond the parameters of these essays. I cite, instead, a near consensus as to the results, as follows:

- First, this was an age of exciting and challenging developments in Hellenistic thought, early developments of Epicureanism, Skepticism, Stoicism – each a general school that included a number of outstanding figures.

- Second, Ecclesiastes includes statements, pieces of advice, and analyses parallel to some found in various Greek texts of the time.

- Third, it would be hard to imagine that the author of Ecclesiastes did not have at least minimal knowledge of some of these schools.

- Fourth, the most often cited schools of thought, Stoicism and Epicureanism, share with Kohelet both an almost total reliance on human experience and an initial trust in the power of reason.

- Fifth, nevertheless, in no case can one point to a specific school of thought or to a thinker of which or of whom one could say, "This was the model for Ecclesiastes."

- Finally, in no case has dependence of this author on a foreign source been demonstrated.

In short, he was a man of his era – an era of questioning and of intellectual exploration. Although the possibility of some borrowings does exist, Ecclesiastes does not parallel any Hellenistic school of thought.[88]

Questioning and doubt, indeed, have accompanied religious thought from its earliest stages, and, in fact, many commentators have found some parallels to Ecclesiastes even centuries before its time.[89] That said, it is of some fascination (a term far removed from presumed broad strokes painting "international intellectual trends") that Ecclesiastes was not alone in his era. Within Greek culture, in particular, there was much change in the air, and certainly one must take note that for the first time in Jewish Wisdom literature, "the Sage gives precedence to his 'I,'"[90] similar to the emphases in contemporary Greek culture.[91] The inclusion of observation of the physical world and the strong exclusive emphasis on empirical evidence also seem to parallel Greek developments.

However, one must differentiate between challenges and responses. Unlike his Greek counterparts (if one can call them that), this author was writing within an intellectual framework of ethical monotheism. The expectations of Divinity therein were radically different from those elsewhere, so even if Hellenist intellectuals used experience and analysis to challenge and develop religious beliefs, it was done from different perspectives. Moreover, even if ideas were shared, the framework made them radically different. "Man was the beginning and end of the discussions of the Greeks.... But the God of Israel could not be disposed of so easily."[92]

One curious result of this difference is reflected in the personal reactions of the authors of the Greek texts and the author of Ecclesiastes. "For a Jew, if a man was alone in this world of Chance, where was the God of Abraham, Isaac, and Jacob ... ? Thus for the Jewish sage the discovery of the vanity of the world was not a step to liberation but a confession of despair."[93] Kohelet, then, cries out, loathes his life, and speaks of his anguish, grief, and despondency. The Greeks sought peace through understanding. Kohelet found pain.

3. Particular Complexities in Reading Ecclesiastes

Ecclesiastes includes a number of distinctive challenges. Where appropriate, I highlight instances wherein these challenges have led some commentators astray. I also indicate instances in which this commentary has responded in specific ways to some of the complexities.

3.1. First Complexity: The Voices Present in the Text

Good imaginative literature is multifaceted. In any such work, one expects apparent contradictions, ambiguities, nuance, and an absence of factors that could conceivably explain the text or cast it in a different light. Over and above that, however, in Ecclesiastes there are many voices, even as the text is presented almost entirely by the main character. These voices are never clearly identified. Further, the text reflects experiences of a lifetime, reasonably implying that one might encounter changes in circumstance, thought, affect, and even vocabulary.

3.1A. THE VOICES OF KOHELET

As others[94] have observed, it is helpful to recall the different voices of Kohelet that appear within the book. The following schematic list is neither exhaustive nor authoritative, but is an attempt to isolate voices that can help the reader to appreciate the work:

1. Kohelet the storyteller, who creates a fictive account of himself as if he were once the king of Israel in Jerusalem, conducting an experiment with achievements in life (in chapters 1 and 2), and who possibly creates other tales (4:13–16; 9:13–15).

2. Kohelet the poet, with at least three major identifiable poems (used as markers for his three main units), which are fascinating in their own right (1:4–7; 3:1–8; 12:1–7), and might (at least in the first two cases) have been written earlier and reinterpreted for the purposes of this text.
3. Kohelet the young man – in a general manner of speaking, the younger person who seeks to experience, observe, and test this world.
4. Kohelet the more experienced man, who has reached conclusions concerning what can (and cannot!) be verified in this world, and how one should and should not act.
5. Kohelet the old man, preoccupied with death.
6. Kohelet the teacher, who seeks to guide his readers as to how to live life.
7. Kohelet the Wisdom scholar, heir to centuries of traditional guidance, including axioms, maxims, and so on.
8. Kohelet the Jew, heir to centuries of Israelite/Jewish teaching.

Some of these divisions are artificial and several overlap. At no point does the text, all written as retrospect, identify one voice or the other. In terms of the book, it is the same character, Kohelet, who relates all. This variety does not imply an exchange of opinions, but rather a book compiled in different stages and circumstances of life and from different modes of literary reflection.

Attempts to assign verses (or half verses!) to different personalities have marked some modern efforts. These create an artificial reading and have no basis in the text itself. In one case, an interpretation that forces the text into a dialogue does violence to the Hebrew, and in another, which assigns four separate (lead) personalities as speaking the text, destroys the beauty and complexity of the work. These are examples of a valid insight (complexity) trivialized from the level of great literature down to the level of administration, and they deserve little attention.

3.1B. THE VOICE OF THE NARRATOR (WITH EXCURSUS ON ELIMINATION)

To these voices, the author adds the voice of a narrator,[95] who briefly introduces the book and who, at the end, expresses admiration for Kohelet, along with some implied reservations and disagreements.[a] Over and above the

---

a. One should also attribute "said Kohelet" (7:27) to the narrator, but the reason for that brief insertion is not clear, so the insertion cannot help one to discern the identity of the narrator and his opinions.

differences of approach between these two, the presence of a "narrator" further complicates the work in that one cannot know with certainty whether within the story Kohelet attempted to collect the contents of this book in an organized manner (which the narrator then "presented"), or whether it is implied that the narrator did so.[96] Indeed, the time span, including all of Kohelet's adult life and beyond, adds the complication of the accuracy of memory, whether that of Kohelet or that of the narrator, or both.

Excursus – on excising the voice of the narrator from Ecclesiastes: On seeing the differences between the narrator and Kohelet, too many commentaries conclude that the end of Ecclesiastes was written by an outside hand (or two – or three!).[97] In that regard, it is of some interest that one medieval commentator, who believed that the narrator in fact collected and edited the whole book, once used a plural construct in referring to the narrator: "those who edited the book speak from here on."[98]

Some suggest that the additions were written in order to legitimize the book, even though it is difficult to understand why someone with significant reservations about the work would do so.[99] Furthermore, other books from antiquity include prefaces and endings spoken by a narrator, a different speaker than in the rest of the text. Even at the beginning of the Book of Deuteronomy an anonymous announcer declares it to be the words Moses spoke, and the book ends with a retrospective account of the departed Moses.[100] In what follows I reiterate my contention that both the words of Kohelet and those of the narrator are the work of a single author.

The criteria used by those who would excise this ending from the original book are highly subjective. There is no doubt that the last sentence and a half, by way of example, adds a new emphasis, but that scarcely justifies the claim of a second author. Even Fox, in marshaling arguments for a separate author, adds, "though not conclusively," and he admits that the end section "is a conclusion that reasonably builds on Qohelet's words."[101]

To move to positive arguments, the fact that the narrator represents a different stance befits a book that already includes the different voices of Kohelet. What is the new voice? There is legitimate room for interpretation as to the degree and kind of disagreement between the narrator and Kohelet. Part of that interpretation depends on how one reads the tone of the words, and particularly whether the epilogue's critique of too much thinking and writing of books is a thinly veiled criticism of Kohelet. Practically everything else said in the epilogue echoes something within Kohelet's words, and one must then judge how different the words are owing to the absence of much that made Kohelet unique – the experimentation, the constant frustration, the emptiness of all pursuits, fearing God out of a conviction of arbitrary rule, and so on.

This epilogue is written with a fascinating mix of phrases. Some of these echo the words of Kohelet, as befits the narrator who admired him, and some present new vocabulary and imagery, as befits a distinct speaker. (See the commentary on the epilogue for details.) Kohelet himself had used earlier biblical vocabulary, twisting the phrases into his own image (3:14; 4:17; 5:3ff.; 5:6; 7:20 – see the commentaries). The narrator now does the same thing to Kohelet's words, particularly the terms and phrases "fear God," "command," "everything," "good," "judgment," and "God will call every deed to judgment," using them in ways other than Kohelet did. In these cases, the narrator returns to older, traditional meanings. Thus the author has the narrator approach Kohelet in the same way that he has Kohelet approach earlier sources.

That said, any differences between the narrator and Kohelet are not so great as to undermine the structured conceit that this narrator would want a reader to confront Kohelet's work. Even some of the commentators who suggest that part of the epilogue is an external addition admit that the text does not force them to make such a judgment.[102] In summary, the epilogue should be seen as received, an inherent part of Ecclesiastes, and it confirms the book's being designed to confront varied perspectives.[a] A single author created all.

3.1C. OTHER VOICES (AUTHOR, TRADITION, WISDOM)

1. THE VOICE OF THE AUTHOR. There is an additional voice, probably impossible to identify: the author of Ecclesiastes, who created both Kohelet and the narrator. To a degree, one can legitimately ask what that author's positions were, just as one might ask what Shakespeare thought, over and above the views expressed by his characters. It may be, however, that one can never know the view of an author,[103] particularly when we know nothing of the author apart from the work produced.[b] By way of example, whereas Kohelet is portrayed

a. See section 1.6 on reading this book as an ongoing challenge to one's thinking.
b. Although we might not know the author's views, we can know something of the author – he could not have written the work without being among the educated and skilled literate minority, familiar with traditional texts and Wisdom literature. "Creative," "original," and

as reaching old age, there is no way of knowing the age of the author. (Given how little we can know of an author, some scholars now use the term "implied author" as the most one can describe,[104] and that is the intent of "author" in this commentary.)

2. THE VOICE OF WISDOM LITERATURE. Throughout the Fertile Crescent (roughly, Egypt through Mesopotamia) and across centuries, if not millennia, Wisdom literature was part of the cultural inheritance of many peoples. International in its nature, it was most frequently applied locally (in terms of culture, religion, etc.), but there is a surprising degree of correspondence across societies. (Ecclesiastes always uses the international term "God" for the Deity, never the [specifically Jewish] Tetragrammaton, often translated "Lord.") Schematically, one can speak of longer, contemplative pieces (similar to the Bible's Job or Ecclesiastes) and collections of wise sayings or aphorisms, advice on how to get along in life (similar to Proverbs). Kohelet, who is pictured as a Wisdom teacher, would have been familiar with this literature, and many suggest that at times he cites a well-known piece of advice, which his audience would recognize as such, sometimes to contradict it by another aphorism or by his own stance. To further complicate the picture, such sayings sometimes contradict one another (two English examples – "a stitch in time saves nine"/"haste makes waste"; and "absence makes the heart grow fonder"/"out of sight, out of mind"), being applicable under different circumstances.

3. THE VOICE OF JEWISH TRADITION. Jewish society had evolved, if one includes all of Israelite biblical history, for a thousand years before Kohelet, and he was heir to that literature and tradition. Therein, there are many normative views (often unstated in Ecclesiastes) and specific pieces of literature from which he drew. (The latter are usually cited in notes in this commentary.) In a broad sense, it is that tradition that is Kohelet's a priori assumption as he begins his search for verification of truths in this world.

4. DISTINGUISHING THE VOICES. There can be no unanimity among readers as to the attribution of the verses to particular voices. That does not imply, however, that the attempt to recognize voices is irrelevant.

"daring" are adjectives that come to mind, adjectives that devolve to his character, Kohelet, in the book.

The existence of voices is an essential tool for anyone seeking depth
of meaning in the text, and doubt is as vital to understanding a text
as is certainty.

3.2. Second Complexity: Contradictions

Famously, the words of Kohelet are marked by apparent contradictions, as
already noted in the Talmud and medieval commentaries:[105] among these
are the desirability of wisdom,[a] the value of wealth and pleasure-seeking,[b]
the assessment of women,[c] and even the approach to enjoyment![d] One
medieval commentator[106] noted the following examples: vexation (once said
to be better than laughter...once said to be dwelling among fools); again
vexation (wisdom inherently creates it...one should avoid it); eating and
drinking (advised...but better to go to a house of mourning than a feast);
enjoyment (praised...damned as worthless); wisdom (superior...inferior
to foolishness); life and death (which is the superior status?); afterlife (no
activity there...everything having a time); the wicked (who will be pun-
ished...who might thrive for an extended time); and reward (given to God
fearers...sometimes given to evildoers).

Some perceived contradictions appear consecutively. I cite two examples:
"The fool folds his hands and so consumes his flesh. Better is a handful of tranquility than two fistfuls of the fruit of toil and anguish" (4:5, 6); and "Better
wisdom than strength, but the wisdom of the poor man is scorned, and his
words are not heeded" (9:16).

Across the centuries, varied approaches have been proposed, and I present
these "solutions" schematically.

1. HARMONIZATION. (1) Identical or similar terms mean different things
   in different places. (2) Different statements refer to different contexts.
2. PRIORITIZATION. (1) One statement is said to be the rule; the other,
   the exception. (2) A statement is said to be conditional on other factors,
   not a generalization.
3. APHORISMS. Citations of "standard" views (often well-accepted

a. Compare 1:16–2:1 with 7:12, 19; 10:10.
b. Compare 2:11; 5:17ff.
c. Compare 7:26; 9:9.
d. Compare 2:1 with the many recommendations to find joyous moments.

aphorisms) are then corrected by Kohelet,[107] either by his own words or by citing an alternate aphorism.

4. TENSION. Opposite poles are presented to create a tension, pointing to a meaning in the middle.[108]

5. ELIMINATION. Phrases, verses, or sections are "eliminated" as additions by a pious editor, notes by a later commentator, someone writing glosses to the text, etc.

6. EMENDATION. Problematic texts are corrected by emendation.

7. DIALOGUE. The entire text has been misunderstood and, rather than being a monologue of Kohelet, it is really an ongoing dialogue between Kohelet and the person who wrote the introduction and the epilogue,[109] or a conversation among various individuals.[110]

8. FLAWED THINKING. Some attribute the inconsistencies to a flaw in Kohelet's thinking.

9. EVOLVED THINKING. I have claimed here that some "contradictions" can be attributed to changes in Kohelet's thinking as he got older, these sometimes occurring earlier in the text (he accepts the value of enjoyment rather early) and sometimes later (e.g., the soul returning to God).

Although any of the first six approaches might apply in one case or another, as a pattern all are significantly flawed.[111] I have related to (and rejected) the seventh option at the end of my comments in section 3.1A.

No approach has led to any sort of consensus among commentators on details. By way of example, a recent compendium of suggested external "citations," based on six modern commentaries, cites one hundred verses in total, with agreement among all six on only one-half of one verse, and only another six verses or phrases merit five agreements![112]

It has also been suggested[113] that the issue is, as one might put it, a matter of perspective. The problem is not that Kohelet contradicts himself, but rather that he finds the world to contain much contradiction: "Qohelet is not so much contradicting himself as *observing* contradictions in the world...." Rather than resolve these contradictions, he records them. This approach has gained growing support over the past few years. One finds here, perhaps, a testimony to the insight of Thomas Mann, the early twentieth-century novelist, that "a great truth is a truth whose opposite is also a truth."[114]

Nevertheless, Kohelet's acceptance of contradictions being inherent in the world does not justify the use of the term "absurdity" to describe it. I suggest the more cautionary "incongruity" or "incomprehensibility" within the *observable* world.[115] Further, the persistence of Kohelet's search and the pain he felt in failing would support "incomprehensible," with its emphasis on the observer, rather than "absurd," describing an external phenomenon.

By way of summary: this commentary reflects my understanding that a large number of "contradictions" represent changes in Kohelet's thinking.[a] Further, some "contradictions" are really refinements, such as the two examples (4:5, 6, and 9:7) cited in the paragraph above on adjacent contradictions. I accept other contradictions as an accurate reflection of the world as Kohelet found it,[116] but not necessarily seen as problematic, recalling Thomas Mann's words cited above. Still other contradictions are interpreted here on an ad hoc basis. (Also recall my comment above,[b] that well-accepted aphorisms sometimes conflict with one another.)

Finally, because Ecclesiastes is primarily a narrative, contradictions are perfectly acceptable, whereas they would not be appropriate in a philosophical treatise. As to those who conclude that this is just poor philosophy, the fault is not in Ecclesiastes, but in the interpretations. A life lived in this world not only can find contradictions – it inevitably does. The inherent tensions among contradictory positions mark this work as a living testimony. They also dictate that the reader be open to noting changes within the book and to hearing the different voices of Kohelet.

3.3. Third Complexity: Literary Challenges (Poetry, Original Language)

The author of Ecclesiastes made two choices that further complicate the task of the reader.

3.3A. POETRY AND FIGURES OF SPEECH

Language orders our lives, but can also mask life's complications. Poetry and figures of speech (metaphors, similes, word plays, etc.) are designed in no small part to overcome that limitation of language, allowing for shades

---

a. See section 1.5C reflected in option 9 above.
b. See section 3.1C, the subsection on Wisdom literature.

of meaning, ambiguity, ambivalence, nuance, multivalence, etc. Given that Ecclesiastes deals with issues of significance, religion, and search, among others, it is no surprise that the author occasionally opts for these more colorful, more realistic, and yet less tangible descriptions.

The outstanding example of a metaphor in Ecclesiastes is *hevel*, the term that is the frame around Kohelet's words, and the guiding word therein, here translated as "vapor," but translated elsewhere as "vanity," "breath," "absurdity," et al. Too many translations err by trying to concretize the metaphor. (See section 4.1B below.) Poetry and symbols must be approached in all their complexity, never trivialized. *Hevel* is maintained here as a metaphor, "vapor," the closest English to its denotation. Although metaphors apart from "vapor" are not frequent in the early part of the book, their use increases, and the final poem describing death is a virtual cascade thereof.

3.3B. NEW TERMINOLOGY

The author uses, and possibly coined, a number of terms not found elsewhere in the Bible. Among these are two on which I comment at length below: "Kohelet" (see section 4.1A) and "anguish" (*re'ut ruach*; see section 4.1C).

Some suggest that in an age of emerging philosophy, the author was struggling with a Hebrew language that had not developed its own philosophical terms, and that he was thus forced into this creativity.[117] Among the terms that appear only in Ecclesiastes one finds "concern" (*inyan*), "already" (*kvar*), "void" (*chisaron*), [the phrase] "under the sun," "depravity" (*holeilot*), "advantage" (*yitron*), and "analysis" (*lahag*). Other terms used frequently throughout the Bible take on new meanings, among them "good" (meaning "beneficial"), and on occasion, "failure" ("not on good terms with God"), a word that elsewhere indicates a "sinner."[a]

Some of the language of the book (including but not limited to new terms) is not subject to sharp definition, and some propose that many of the aspects of Ecclesiastes that are less than clear were written that way deliberately,[118] a literary reflection of Kohelet's central contention that one cannot understand God's work.[119] That kind of literary sophistication did exist in biblical literature, so one can imagine that the author used terms and phrases in that way.[120] The question, of course, is moot, but it is sufficiently seductive to merit mention.

a. See section 4.2 below.

4. Decisions Reflected in This Commentary: Translations

Any translation is ipso facto an interpretation. Therefore, I clarify some of the choices made in this translation, sometimes detailing their justification. I first focus on three central words, "Kohelet," "vapor," and "anguish," and then proceed to other basic terms. (The extensive comments on "vapor" are divided into subparagraphs.) I then comment on other aspects of the translation (e.g., Hebrew text and the emphasis on "I").

4.1. Three Central Terms: "Kohelet," "Vapor," and "Anguish"

4.1A. "KOHELET" (ALSO EXPLAINING "ECCLESIASTES")

Throughout this commentary, the term "Ecclesiastes" refers to the book in its entirety, and the term "Kohelet" (a Hebrew name) refers to the persona who is the principal speaker. This Hebrew root (*k-h-l*) means "to gather," which in the Bible refers exclusively to assembling people. Beginning with some medieval commentators, it has been suggested that "gathering" refers to objects (sayings)[121] or to wisdom itself.[122]

There is no agreement regarding the name's exact interpretation. It may indicate a role (possibly professional), hence the occasional preference of translators for "preacher" or "teacher." It may even indicate an official role, as court positions in some societies were labeled by profession. Twice in biblical texts from the Second Temple period a similar grammatical form is used as a personal name reference,[123] possibly indicating that the professional title evolved into a name (e.g., modern "Butch" from butcher and Paige from court page).[a]

a. The phenomenon is more familiar from family names, a modern development, such as Baker, Taylor, and Cook, among others.

"Kohelet" appears seven times, once with the definite pronoun (as if it were to read "the Kohelet," 12:8). Further, that verse is one of three in which the phrase "Kohelet said" appears, but they all read slightly differently. If one were to translate literally, they would read: "Kohelet [he] said" (1:2); "Kohelet [she] said" (7:27), and "the Kohelet [he] said" (12:8). Scholars frequently suggest emendation in order to make these texts uniform, and some hold the inclusion of the definite article (which might appear twice if one accepts a proposed emendation of 7:27) to hint at the original interpretation of the word as a profession. Others even suggest that the confusion of these three verses is a purposeful technique to obscure the identity of the speaker.[124]

Uncertainty leads most modern translators to use the transliteration, Kohelet, as done here. ("Ecclesiastes" is an early guess at the meaning, indicating a member of the "gathering," that is, community, and is the Latin translation of the title given the book in Greek.) In transliterating, some use "Q" for "K," and some use "th" for "t."

The uncertainty of the name's implication has allowed for several far-flung suggestions, including one who gathered Wisdom scholars together[125] and a speaker who really represents a chorus of identifiable personalities.[126] One commentator[127] reinterprets verses into an ongoing dialogue between the narrator and Kohelet. In terms of the volumes identifying different personalities, one should take heed of the comment made by Ibn Ezra on 7:3, that "one commentator interpreted Kohelet as Kehilat Yaakov (the congregation of Jacob], saying that his students wrote the book, each expressing his own opinion – but this is totally incorrect!"[128] His comment still holds true, and I repeat from the section above on the voices of Kohelet that these approaches are examples of a valid insight (complexity) trivialized from the level of great literature down to the level of administration. That said, the claim[129] that the uncertainty about the name, like other uncertainties in the book, is reflective of the world's incomprehensibility has much to recommend it.

4.1B. "VAPOR" (HEVEL)

I. INTRODUCTION. The guide-word of Ecclesiastes, *hevel* (translated here as "vapor"), has engendered volumes of discussion and analysis. In what follows I discuss the meaning of the term, its uses, a general approach to metaphors, and specific suggestions concerning the term *hevel*.

II. THE CORE MEANING. Uses in the Bible and in cognate languages indicate that the denotation of the *hevel* is approximately "vapor" or "exhalation." This is reflected in Isaiah 57:13 ("snatched away by a breeze," parallel to "taken by *hevel*") and Psalm 62:10 (a poor man and rich man together weigh less than a *hevel*). It bears some similarity to the modern term "nonentity," which wavers between "not existing at all" and "of no import."

III. USES ELSEWHERE IN THE BIBLE. There are forty uses of the root *hevel* elsewhere in the Bible, all symbolic,[130] with prime reference to its connotations: physical and temporal insubstantiality. One commentator, in his summary of non-Ecclesiastes applications, lists (other than its denotation), in descending order of the number of uses: a term for idols (sixteen times), worthless/false, no purpose/useless, futile, nothing/empty, fleeting, and deceptive in appearance. He concludes that all these uses are judgmental and negative.[131]

IV. THE USES IN ECCLESIASTES. *Hevel* is used five times in 1:2 and three times in 12:8, these verses being the framework for Kohelet's words. In these two verses, the multiple repetition, two other echoing terms, and the shocking use of the superlative form for a negative phenomenon (see the commentary) all dramatically emphasize the term. If the Song of Songs was a known work[132] by that time, it is conceivable that the author of Ecclesiastes was punning it, perhaps assuming that his work would be known as "Vapor of Vapors."

The term appears another thirty-one times, and clearly the reader is meant to hear the resounding repetition. There is a major difference between the use of *hevel* elsewhere and here. Elsewhere the description "vapor" is always of a *thing* (or used for breath as a simile, as in Psalm 39), whereas the author of Ecclesiastes both adopted and adapted the metaphor, because here in the majority of cases *situations* are described as "vapor."[133]

V. METAPHOR IN GENERAL AND IN ECCLESIASTES. In recent decades, scholars have tended to abandon the once firm differentiation between "live" and "dead" metaphors. ("Dead" or "stock" metaphors are those so commonly used that one is oblivious to the term's original implication, such as the modern "hands of a clock," "legs of a chair," and "strong coffee.") Whether the division still holds or not, within Ecclesiastes this metaphor breathes and lives (to use a metaphor). At first Ecclesiastes is not dominated by live metaphors.

However, these (with similes) increase as the book nears its end, culminating in a virtual cascade of metaphors in the final poem.[a]

In terms of metaphors in general, little is gained by seeking to interpret them (i.e., indicate their implication) through translation,[134] apart from such instances wherein modern usage of the denotation would lead a reader astray. Most readers are capable of imagining the range of possible implications of a metaphor as literally presented.

In most uses in Ecclesiastes *hevel* describes a pronoun or noun, often "this" and sometimes "all/everything." The referent for "this" in most of these contexts, however, is vague, usually summarizing a series of observations or activities or a combination thereof. Thus, analyzing the implication of the metaphor in many instances is doubly complex

VI. APPROACHES TO TRANSLATING HEVEL. Miller[135] has tried to make sense of the various translations of *hevel* by grouping approaches into three categories: (a) an abstraction (such as "absurd," "meaningless," "transient," "vain/vanity"), with one chosen term used for all translations; (b) multiple translations (implying multiple, distinct implications); and (c) "single metaphor" (one term that has a single meaning that covers all occurrences). The approach in this commentary befits the third category.[136] I now comment on the three categories, the third to be discussed via the term chosen in this commentary – "vapor."

VII. MULTIPLE TRANSLATIONS. Translating differently[137] in each case is clearly the least satisfactory approach to translating *hevel*, for it does not allow the English reader to follow repeated uses. In that regard, Fox writes of others' use of many terms: "To do Qohelet justice, we must look for a concept that applies to all occurrences."[138] He and others are particularly concerned that the reader appreciate the summarizing quality of the framing opening and closing passages, which depends on the use of a single term.

VIII. TRANSLATION, BY IMPLICATION, TO AN ABSTRACT NOUN. It has been noted that "Vapor in itself is a multipurpose metaphor," and "the meaning of *hevel* must be derived from context."[139] Those determinations should be enough to keep interpreters from seeking a single term based on implication. Nevertheless, many do so, most often choosing an abstract quality. Since the

---

a. See the commentary in part III, 12:1–7, and section 1.5B in these essays.

advent of the King James Bible, the preferred English has often been "vanity." (Other suggestions include "nothingness," "futility," "meaningless," and "senselessness."[140]) Among the difficulties in this approach is the fact that no abstraction holds in all cases.

A second difficulty is the general principle that metaphors are best represented by themselves (as seen above). In arguing for an abstraction, one interpreter[141] cites the example of 8:14 (noting that the righteous sometimes receive what is due the wicked and vice versa, which is called *hevel*), saying that to call this vapor(ous) gives "no information about it." But that is, of course, the beauty of metaphors. They dramatically present possible implications, and sometimes a range thereof. In the verse in question, it is up to the reader to sense how the insubstantiality of vapor applies to the described situation (quite possibly, the frustration of not being able to get a hold of it). This is not "information about" the described situation, but a reaction to it.

A further word is due on another frequently suggested abstraction, "absurdity," over and above both the preference for the denotation and the admission that no translation holds for every occurrence.[142] In suggesting "absurdity," Fox (the foremost proponent of the usage) defines "absurdity" on the basis of the writings of Albert Camus, in which "the feeling of absurdity...bursts from the comparison between a bare fact and a certain reality."[143] That is not quite what happens in Ecclesiastes, wherein Kohelet is seeking empirical evidence for values and beliefs. The two described situations might be too close to be realistically divided, were it not for the fact that Kohelet clearly comes to the conclusion that his powers of observation and analysis are not up to the task – that is to say, if he finds no empirical evidence, the problem is not inherently in the condition of the thing observed but possibly in the limited eye of the beholder.[144] That possibility makes the choice of the term "absurd" somewhat absurd.

There is indeed a term for the situation Fox describes, which is "incomprehensibility." However, Fox rejects that, noting that "'Incomprehensible' indicates that the meaning of a phenomenon is opaque to human intellect and allows for, and may even suggest, that it is actually meaningful and significant. To call something 'absurd,' on the other hand, is to claim some knowledge about its quality."[145]

That is correct (apart from the gratuitous "and may even suggest" – it does no such thing)! If one were to seek an abstraction, "incomprehensible" would be the term best suited.[146] However, as stated, an abstraction is not to be preferred to the original denotation, "vapor," to which I now proceed.

IX. THE TRANSLATION "VAPOR." For all the reasons detailed above, the preferred translation of *hevel* is "vapor," its denotation, understanding that it carries with it the connotations, as present throughout the Bible, of insubstantiality in time and place. One might try to combine the denotation and connotations in translating, particularly for the summary phrase, "vapor of vapors." One such option might be "dust in the wind," the title and central phrase of a song by guitarist Kerry Livgren of the band Kansas.[a] One could also consider a "breath in a breeze." Neither of these, however, replicates the Hebrew repetition, and they are too awkward for use in standard translations.

I also note the three "qualities" of the symbol *hevel* in Ecclesiastes as suggested by another commentator: insubstantiality, transience, and foulness.[147] The question here is methodological. These "qualities" of the metaphor were discovered by observing terms that are "guards," that is, nearby similar descriptions. Of the three, however, the first two are clearly the word's connotations and need no such support. "Foul" is based on these "guards," but if one assumes, as I do, that these added phrases (often the term "debilitating") do not parallel "vapor" but *add* to it, "vapor" itself does not change. It remains "a multipurpose metaphor" to be constantly re-appreciated.

X. THE METAPHOR AS ITS USE CHANGES. Of some interest are the changes within the patterns of use of "vapor" in the book. Through the voice of the narrator, "vapor" is the framing term of Ecclesiastes (1:2; 12:8), but within that framework there is a pattern of decreasing use in Kohelet's words. Many of the occurrences are found within the pseudo-autobiography (in chapter 2) and the usage lessens as the text moves on.[148] Moreover, the uses of "vaporous" referring to the days of one's (his/mine/your) life are all in the second half (6:12; 7:15; 9:9). This last phenomenon almost certainly reflects the growing personalization of the book.

Thus the framing summary may lead us astray. If the words of Kohelet within that frame were written and ordered by him and reflect growth, then as he progressed in preparing the manuscript, he became less enamored of the word, but more likely to apply it to the (fleeting!) days of life, as opposed

a. The phrase was taken from a Native American poem.

to using it to refer to what he observed in the world. The narrator, who uses "vapor of vapors" to summarize the beginning and the end, would be depicted by the author as either having been unaware of this evolvement or, alternatively, as celebrating it by ironically using the same phrase at both points, even though the implications were ever so slightly different.

4.1C. "ANGUISH"

A thick veil surrounds *re'ut ruach* (which also appears twice in an alternative form, *ra'ayon ruach*[149]), a phrase unique to Ecclesiastes. The first word of the pair might be related to different base meanings and roots in either Hebrew or Aramaic (including "bad," "break," "pursue" [like a shepherd], "thought," or "desire"), the second term can mean "breath," "wind," or "spirit," and the phrase is translated by a wide variety of terms.[150]

Most modern translations opt for versions of "chasing the wind," partially because of its frequent appearance together with "vapor." Variations include "grasping after…," "striving for…," and "feeding on the wind." Methodologically this reflects a preference for the assumption that vapor and *re'ut ruach* have parallel meanings. However, it is at least equally logical to assume that this phrase adds to the meaning of "vapor," rather than just emphasizing it, particularly in that "vapor" calls for added references to bolster its connotation of "insubstantiality." Further, "vapor" continues to appear after the middle of the book, but not so *re'ut ruach*, supporting the contention that this phrase is to be distinguished from "vapor."

In the present commentary, I follow, approximately, several ancient translations and early commentators[151] who seem to base themselves on the root meanings "breaking" and "spirit," and I translate the term as "anguish." As noted, the phrase disappears as the book progresses.[a] As a wordplay, the phrase remains related through the first word, *re'ut*, to Ecclesiastes's frequent use of r-'-' as "evil" ("bad," "detrimental," "calamity" – see below).

Further, it might have been legitimate, in the case of this phrase, given the lack of clarity, to opt for a translation that somehow bridges suggestions, even if it does not actually match any of them. One such term might be "frustration," an inevitable result of "chasing the wind" or "having senseless desires" and a term approximating "anguish." I have not done so because

---

a. See section 1.5A.

there is little chance that the author sought to imply multiplicity in this case. That technique is appropriate for words that are well known, but this is a new phrase, and therefore one must use his or her understanding of the book as a whole to seek the most likely translation.

4.2. Other Basic Terms (Alphabetical English Order)

BAD, EVIL, DETRIMENT, CALAMITY. All of these represent a single Hebrew root, r-'-', which is repeated twenty-eight times (independent of any relationship to "anguish," as detailed in the paragraphs immediately above).[152]

CALAMITY. See above, "bad."

DETRIMENT. See above, "bad."

DOLT. See below, "fool."

EVIL. See above, "bad."

FAIL(URE). Used often as the opposite of "good" (see below), this term (ch-t-') elsewhere in the Bible indicates sin. As has been recognized, it is sometimes used in Ecclesiastes to reflect its core meaning, "miss the mark." It indicates one who falls out of favor with God, not necessarily implying a moral fault.[153]

FOOL AND DOLT. These two terms are used interchangeably by Kohelet and have almost identical roots, by metathesis [reversal of letters]: in Hebrew, s-ch-l and ch-s-l.

GOOD [BETTER, BEST], BENEFIT [BENEFICENCE]. "Good" (tov) is almost always used from the perspective of man, that is, what is of benefit to him, not what is "virtuous," ethically right, or commanded.[154] (It is close to "effective" behavior.) This is so even concerning the term "tov before God" ("good in God's presence"; 2:26; 7:26), indicating "fortunate enough to merit God's beneficence."[155]

SEE. This often repeated term (forty-three uses) has a range similar to its meaning in English, including physical sight, taking notice, understanding, experiencing, and observing.

TOIL. Amal, an earlier biblical term indicating in Hebrew a degree of (experiencing or causing) suffering, here (and only in Ecclesiastes) denotes difficult labor, hence "toil." The term is used both for the toil itself and, as a metonym, the resulting wealth or possessions, and it is sometimes used twice in the same phrase with those two implications. To maintain that echo, I occasionally translate with a partial rhyme, "spoils of one's toil." (On occasion it is unclear whether Kohelet is questioning the value of the toil or of the wealth.) When *amal* appears alone as a metonym for "wealth," I translate it as "fruit of one's toil."

UNDER THE SUN. This phrase, found only in Ecclesiastes, occurs at least once in every section. (A similar phrase used elsewhere in the Bible, "under the heavens," appears three times.) Its use in other ancient languages indicates both inclusivity (all the area mentioned) and exclusivity (the land of the living, either spatially or, often, temporally, that is, as opposed to after death).[156]

I suggest that the Bible has an additional frame of reference that informs the use here. In Genesis 1 God creates the universe by dividing the waters above and those below by the heavens, in which He places the sun. Further, many other biblical verses locate God in or above the heavens[a] (although He clearly functions in heaven and on earth), including Ecclesiastes 5:1. "Under the sun" would indicate that Kohelet does not discuss the part of the universe he cannot experience. The book gives yet another clue to the import of the phrase in some of its uses of "darkness." In 6:4, 11:8, and 12:2 the reference may be to death, in the last of these verses in direct opposition to "sun." This accords with the use of the phrase in other languages. In sum, the term "under the sun" spans all time and space *exclusive of* anything unknown to man.[157]

There may be further motives for choosing this phrase ("under the sun"). It may be related to Kohelet's emphasis on "seeing" (i.e., observing and understanding). Longman suggests that "the choice of . . . *under the sun* rather than the more prosaic 'on earth' intends to appeal to the imagination of the reader in a memorable way."[158] Perhaps the phrase also communicates the discomfort of Kohelet's perspective by invoking an image of sweltering heat.[159] In any case, what Kohelet finds to be "vapor," is "under the sun," that is, in the empirical world.[160]

4.3. Other Aspects of Translation

The following additional decisions were basic to this translation.

---

a. For example, Psalms 18:10, 14; 57:6; 113:4; and 115:16.

REPETITION. On occasion, a part of the Bible should be translated using (if possible) a single parallel term in the translation for each Hebrew term.[161] Two factors make that very difficult in Ecclesiastes. First, the text is a retrospective collection of pieces composed over a lifetime and it includes different voices (as discussed above), even if edited. Second, the author eschews close development of a single term, possibly a literary reflection of his contention that rules and patterns are ultimately indiscernible. He is in this manner rejecting a literary biblical convention, that is, the development of a central term as a prime indicator of meaning. Nevertheless, I try to maintain a single translation (even at the cost of mellifluousness) for each Hebrew term, but am forced on occasion to use varied translations.[a] In the latter cases, when it seems that there is a purposeful echo, I have so noted in the commentary. English terms, on the other hand, each reflect only one Hebrew term, and repeated uses may be pondered by the reader.

"I." In Hebrew the first-person singular can be a self-standing pronoun or a suffix, nominal or verbal. I choose to repeat "I" when the text uses both a pronoun and a suffix, an emphasis on the individual speaker that I feel is intended, given the unusual reliance on personal experience in this text.[162] There are more than twenty such double uses in Ecclesiastes.[163]

SUBJECT-VERB AGREEMENT. The Hebrew includes several instances wherein a singular noun takes a plural verb and vice versa. I translate literally unless the phrasing becomes particularly awkward.

DOUBLE ROOT. When the Hebrew uses the same root twice in a sentence (which classical Hebrew frequently does), I often reflect the literal Hebrew as opposed to using more colloquial English (e.g., "a single destiny is destined," not "a single destiny is set" and "accomplishments accomplished," not "accomplishments achieved").

PROSE OR POETRY? The line between prose and poetry in biblical Hebrew is not sharp, and there are significant differences among translations of Ecclesiastes as to which verses are printed as each. Those sections, including pithy aphorisms, that seem to be best understood as poetic in form, are indented

---

a. This is particularly true of the most commonly used words. By way of example, ʿ-s-h is variously translated "do," "create," "act," "accomplish," "work," and "asset."

within the text. However, many verses might be seen as either prose or poetry, and the decision is sometimes almost arbitrary.

SOURCE. This translation follows the Masoretic (authoritative Hebrew) text. Any variation is detailed in the notes. When the Masoretic text presents two alternatives (*ktiv* – as printed; *kri* – as it is to be read), I usually follow the majority of previous commentators, often without further comment.

5. Decisions Reflected in This Commentary: Subdividing Ecclesiastes

5.1. Guiding Principles and Overview

The chapter division of Ecclesiastes (as is the case with all books of the Bible) is a late phenomenon (attributed to Stephen Langton, archbishop of Canterbury, 1217). That division cannot be assumed to reflect the original intent of the author. The question remains: Are there, in fact, subdivisions of the book?

The division of Ecclesiastes is one of the greatest challenges facing an interpreter, and there is simply no consensus. So difficult is the issue that the title of the most detailed proposal used a metaphor: "the riddle of the Sphinx."[164] The many repetitions and apparent contradictions, as well as the lack of consistent time progression, militate against easy division. Furthermore, the "markers" used in other books (e.g., differing guide words, framing terminology, refrains, or ongoing sharp changes of focus) overlap and fail to define meaningful or helpful divisions. Many commentators have given up on the effort or have ended up with so many small divisions that one has difficulty following the work as a whole.[165] However, once the book is seen as a narrative rather than a philosophical tract, it is possible to detect a loose structure that not only guides reading, but also clarifies several basic elements of the book. It is my view that the literary structure of prime importance is reflected in the book's three units, which I have titled parts I, II, and III.

Immediately after the narrator's opening announcement (1:1–2), one finds a hermetically sealed part I. On the outer extremes (1:3 and 3:9), there are nearly identical rhetorical questions ("what advantage can a man gain?"). After the first and before the second rhetorical question are two powerful poems, one dwelling on the world's eternal lack of change and one on the inability of man to control events. Between these two poems there is an autobiographical section, wherein Kohelet details his "experiment" with various goals, none of which he finds to be inherently worthwhile. This unit is the grand opening of the book.[166]

In the longer part II, Kohelet observes others, not himself, seeking evidence of God's functioning in the world, and again he fails to find it. This unit integrates observation and advice, and the unit is divisible into sections on the basis of a themed repetition that serves as an ending refrain.[167] This is Kohelet's insight that the best one can do is to find some enjoyment in life (a theme that also appeared in part I in 2:24–26 and in 3:12–13, and reappears at the beginning of part III in 11:9). That insight, which evolves from observation to admonition as the book progresses, is found in part II in 3:22; 5:19; 7:14,[168] 8:15; 9:7–10; and 11: 8, each marking the end of one of its six sections. Further, at or near the beginning of each section one finds the term "see," which also appears at the end of the unit, in 11:7, closing it off.[a]

Each section in part II also contains at least one "core" term, a term that appears there in a plurality of its uses within the book, that is, more times within that section than in any other (as divided here). To clarify: such a term is not used exclusively in that section, nor does it necessarily dominate it. Rather, the sections reflect a more spontaneous flow, with repetitions and digressions hinting at emotional associations or the origin of the work as a collection that stretches over many years. These core terms are noted below in the review of the sections.

The idea that "enjoyment" defines these subsections has been made once before,[169] but has not been widely accepted. I believe the principal reason is that scholars are looking for too much in the structure and/or seeking a treatise-like division.[170] However, this being a narrative, experientially based (but not consecutive) and retrospective, the division seems logical enough, and certainly aids the reader. The final unit, part III, is a poem reflecting man's end (death). As the end of Kohelet's words, it is a tragic balance to the eternity and unchangeable pattern of the universe in the opening unit, part I.

Following these three units there is an epilogue by the narrator.

---

a. "See" is used in many other contexts. It is "enjoyment" that delimits the sections.

5.2. A Schematic Presentation of the Book's Divisions

The following represents the divisions of the Book of Ecclesiastes as I understand it.

The Narrator Looking Forward – An Introduction. The opening title and summary (1:1–2).

Kohelet's Words Part I: My Life as King. A pseudo-autobiography of Kohelet as a king, surrounded by two poems interpreted to say that man can gain no advantage in this world. The three sections are as follows:

1. The Song of Sun and Wind. The opening poem, interpreted to reflect the immutability and incomprehensibility of existence (1:3–11).

2. Trial and Failure. The tale of the king and his experiment (1:12–2:26).

3. The Song of Times and Seasons. The closing poem, interpreted to show that man cannot effect change (3:1–15).

Kohelet's Words Part II: The Choices of Life. The long middle unit: observation of, and advice to, others. The six sections are

1. Everything Equal, Everything Evil. A personal plaint: omnipresent evil, humans no different than animals (3:16–22), the core term being "everything" (hakol).

2. Society as Failure. Sociologically based complaints, with Kohelet's first inclusion of advice (4:1–5:19), the core terms being "toil/spoils," "see," and "under the sun" (all emphasizing human society).

3. The "Best" You Can Do. The height of depressed complaint, in that wealth brings no benefit, with a response; there are, comparatively, some pursuits and attitudes that are superior to others (6:1–7:14), and the core term is "good/better/beneficial."

4. Lost at Seeing. A single observation (the absence of justice, which encloses the section) leads to immediate advice, and the section then seems to draw heavily on direct experience (7:15–8:15), with the core term being "find/discover."

5. Toward Love and Life. A depressed view of the absence of clear knowledge, and nondifferentiated fate, but including two reverses: a preference for life over death and a recommendation to love (8:16–9:10), the core term being "life/living."

6. Calculations, True and False. With hints again of autobiography, this section focuses on unrewarding efforts, leading to advice of playing it safe and, of course, enjoying what can be enjoyed (9:11–11:8); the core term is "wisdom."

Kohelet's Words Part III: Death and Enjoyment. Finale. The two sections are as follows:

1. Take Joy When You Can, When Young. Again, the default best option: enjoyment, here opening part III (11:9–10).

2. The Song of Old Age and Death. The closing poem of old age and death (12:1–12:7).

The Narrator, Looking Back – An Epilogue. Restates the theme and adds admiration for, and disagreement with, Kohelet (12:8–14).

This division is by no means hermetic, but it does allow the reader to progress through the book more easily and does correspond to certain of the author's emphases. As the text goes on, some observations are repeated and suggestions are restated. As this is literature, such repetitions are fully understandable and possibly reveal the concerns that most occupied Kohelet.

6. Decisions Reflected in This Commentary: Four Roads Not Taken

In what follows I discuss four emphases found with some frequency in contemporary commentaries, but absent from the present work, clarifying why I have not pursued them.

6.1. Ambiguity

With increasing frequency over recent years, scholars make reference to the "ambiguity" of Ecclesiastes. However, that description is used in such different ways that it is advisable to avoid it, if only on those grounds. I proceed to deal with some of the varied implications of "ambiguity."

Some modern theories of reading would deny (all or almost all) inherent meaning to any written text, locating *both* meaning and significance within the reader. Simplistically put (and all will excuse, I hope, this crude summary), this "reader-response theory" in its most radical formats would inherently call any text ambiguous.[171] Rather than enter that complex debate on the degree of inherent meaning, I simply clarify that I feel that to some degree the text does define limits and meaning, and it does so unambiguously. Many interpretations may be acceptable, but some are not. Any good commentary should proceed by both determining what the text says unambiguously and by helping readers find the markers to respond to in discerning meaning beyond that. "Meaning is not to be found either in the reader or in the text, but emerges in the interaction between the two."[172]

Even within the realm of accepting limits within the text, there is sharp difference among commentators on two questions: whether Ecclesiastes is "ambiguous," and if so, is that a good or a bad thing? To deal with those questions, one must first clarify the term. Basically, a word, phrase, sentence, etc., might be said to be ambiguous if it has more than one possible meaning, particularly if there are no tools available to determine definitively which of those is "right" or "intended" or "appropriate."

The claim that "Ecclesiastes is ambiguous"[173] can refer to the whole or to its parts. As a complete work, it seemingly is open to an unusually wide range of interpretations. In terms of its parts, there seem to be a large number of details or sections that can be so described. Indeed, many relate the two, the wide use of specific ambiguity leading to the ambiguity of the whole (although other factors, such as the contradictions discussed above, also contribute).

I first relate to ambiguous details: Is Ecclesiastes relatively radical in its *number* of ambiguities? Supporting that contention would be the significant number of new terms that seem to be at least a little unclear, as well as some of the metaphors.[174] The three major poems in the book are certainly ambiguous (that is the nature of much poetry). Nevertheless, the book when judged by its details is not nearly as ambiguous as volumes that are wholly poetry, nor is it as ambiguous as those biblical books that rest heavily on citations from earlier texts (e.g., Ruth, Esther, and several psalms), which always have many possible explanations. In short, if the phrase "Ecclesiastes is ambiguous" implies "more so than any other biblical text," it probably misses the mark.

As to the text as a whole being ambiguous, much depends on what the expectations are. If a clearly stated philosophy is sought, Ecclesiastes is unabashedly ambiguous. If, however, the purpose of this book (as seen above) is rather to be a goad to further thought by offering challenges, the expectations reduce the ambiguity. Moreover, as the book is a narrative, much is held back from the reader, as is typical of that genre, leaving out wide swaths of information, "gaps" to be filled.

Further, to the degree that ambiguity is present, if one "message" of Ecclesiastes (or of Kohelet) is that the world is "incomprehensible," then many of the ambiguities become a reflection of that truth, the form being (unambiguously!) a reinforcement of content. This would be "positive" ambiguity, joining other usages that are positive – particularly the challenging metaphors (such as "vapor"), multivalence, and open questions.

There are also many ways in which Ecclesiastes is *not* ambiguous.[a]

a. Any reader is himself part of the process of interacting with a text, and so it is very difficult to separate out those elements that one feels are inherent to the text and those that s/he has read in. That said, I would still state what follows.

Ecclesiastes unambiguously defines itself as a work of imagination. Kohelet unambiguously depends on experience and observation (i.e., vicarious experience) as his source of empirical truth in the seeable world, as he unambiguously confines his comments to that world ("under the sun"). He unambiguously finds that all is incomprehensible (a prime implication of "vapor"). He unambiguously recommends enjoyment where it can be had and offers other pieces of advice. The author unambiguously indicates that change occurred in Kohelet's thinking, particularly as he grew older. Ecclesiastes unambiguously suggests that Kohelet's view is controversial.

As a narration, then, Ecclesiastes records its story clearly. But there is much we do not know about Kohelet and his environment. If this leaves the reader with insufficient information to conclude what the full nature of the text's religious thought was (or even just Kohelet's), or what further recommendations would be, then the reader has read well. If the reader is frustrated thereby, the author possibly achieved his purpose. If any of that can be called ambiguity (an issue that has boiled down to a moot question of semantics), may it be blessed!

6.2. Pessimism

"Ecclesiastes...is known in world literature for its pessimism," begins one modern commentary,[175] and another remarks on "the author's mood of... pessimism,"[176] a description found in many other works on Ecclesiastes.

"Optimism" is usually understood to imply positive anticipations and expectations, and pessimism the opposite. If one discusses the chances of a person discovering the hand of justice, logic, and so on in the visible universe, then, indeed, the character Kohelet is pessimistic, but only at the end of his observations and experiments. However, if one discusses what is *expected* to happen tomorrow or at any time in the future, the more exact response is that Kohelet would say that he does not know – rules are undiscoverable at best; the world seems incomprehensible! Ecclesiastes's challenge is the inability to know, not the lack of promise of a better day tomorrow. Even concerning understanding – at the end he is *certain* that he will not find it, not pessimistic about finding it. It is therefore preferable not to use the term "pessimism," which only obfuscates.

6.3. Absurdity

Taken by the possible similarity of Kohelet's thought to that of Albert Camus, some commentators (prominently among them, Fox) hold that "vapor" should be translated as "absurd(ity)," reflecting what they consider to be the main thrust of that metaphor in Ecclesiastes. I have written at length in various places in these Review Essays on the preference for translating a metaphor by its denotation (here, "vapor") and have detailed numbers of other reasons to maintain that translation in this case (see 5.1B above). Over and above the translation, however, the question remains as to whether the world's absurdity is a central message of Ecclesiastes as a whole, or even of the character Kohelet.

The term as commonly conceived is a negative ("ridiculously senseless... contrary to all reason or common sense" – Webster's Universal Dictionary), and whereas the text borders on this, it is simply not quite that extreme. The world is unpredictable, and one cannot discover there the verification of values of wisdom, religious tradition, or widely held assumptions, but that is less than "contrary to all reason and common sense."[177] A less judgmental term, such as "incomprehensible," is much to be preferred, and does not impose upon the text a step that it does not take. Furthermore, "incomprehensible" implies that the shortcoming may be partially in the *observable* world and partially in other factors, in particular, the limitations of the observer.

6.4. The Sounds of Silence

Finally, one must, given other commentaries, recall the precaution that the reader should not draw conclusions about the book from what is not said. There are always many possible explanations as to why something was not included within any work. Silence does not testify to a specific conclusion drawn by the commentator.

One conclusion often so erroneously drawn about Kohelet is his lack of concern for the downtrodden. Statements such as "Kohelet's failure to respond actively to social injustice and political tyranny constitutes a crucial defect"[178] simply have no basis. The author was not writing about achieving social justice or equity, but rather about Kohelet's search for verifiable life choices and about how one might go on given their absence. He was not detailing all of what one was to do in life (and indeed, Kohelet's demand that one fear God may encompass much social concern, given the tradition to which he was heir and within which the author wrote).

The second error that derives from silence, on which I have focused frequently, is the tendency to over-interpret and to read matters into Ecclesiastes that it does not include. Hence, there is a markedly wide range of summaries of the book.[179] There is evidently a human tendency to read in more than the text says – most often, one's own positions. Although this can be one way to extract benefit from the text, still one must step back and acknowledge, as I noted above, that meaning lies between the book and the reader, and is not inherent in the text.

It is therefore worthwhile to end by repeating what I wrote above in the section on content: Ecclesiastes is not a prescription for all of one's life, but a demand for what one must *include* in one's thinking. It is a book that ends not with a "!" but with a "?!" It is not an answer to all challenges, but a challenge to all answers.[180]

7. Appendix: Literary Reactions to Ecclesiastes

In view of how much of world literature takes up the themes of Ecclesiastes, any attempt to provide a comprehensive survey of reactions to this great book is doomed to failure. As early as 1888, Plumptre[a] appended to his commentary some forty pages of reflections on this work – and he related *only* to Shakespeare and Tennyson!

I include below a few works that react directly to Ecclesiastes. None of these pieces was written in consideration of the preceding commentary, but they all touch upon relevant matters. They are presented in consideration of my conviction that Ecclesiastes was written in order to spur further thinking. Certainly the pieces that follow reflect that, and several express strong disagreement. To repeat Thomas Mann's insight, "A great truth is a truth whose opposite is also a truth."[b]

I clarify that the selections were not chosen owing to any personal association with the authors or their perspectives. None of these sources was originally written in English, and many are not readily available, so in part they are a service to the English-speaking audience, which might be less familiar with them.

a. E.H. Plumptre, *Ecclesiastes; or The Preacher* (Cambridge, UK: Cambridge University Press, 1888), pp. 231–68.
b. In Mann's essay on Freud, delivered October 16, 1929, and often cited, including in Shapira, p. 32.

Wislawa Szymborska: "To Chat with the Ecclesiastes"[a]

Speech on Receipt of Nobel Prize for Literature, 1996
Translation: Stanislaw Baranczak and Clare Cavanagh

I sometimes dream of situations that can't possibly come true. I audaciously imagine, for example, that I get a chance to chat with the Ecclesiastes, the author of that moving lament on the vanity of all human endeavors. I would bow very deeply before him, because he is, after all, one of the greatest poets, for me at least.

That done, I would grab his hand. "'There's nothing new under the sun': that's what you wrote, Ecclesiastes. But you yourself were born new under the sun. And the poem you created is also new under the sun, since no one wrote it down before you. And all your readers are also new under the sun, since those who lived before you couldn't read your poem. And that cypress that you're sitting under hasn't been growing since the dawn of time. It came into being by way of another cypress similar to yours, but not exactly the same.

"And Ecclesiastes, I'd also like to ask you what new thing under the sun you're planning to work on now? A further supplement to the thoughts you've already expressed? Or maybe you're tempted to contradict some of them now? In your earlier work you mentioned joy – so what if it's fleeting? So maybe your new-under-the-sun poem will be about joy? Have you taken notes yet, do you have drafts? I doubt you'll say, 'I've written everything down, I've got nothing left to add.' There's no poet in the world who can say this, least of all a great poet like yourself."

R. Yosef Tzvi Carlebach: "The Pessimism of Liberation"[b]

The following excerpt is from Rabbi Carlebach's introduction to his commentary on Ecclesiastes, written in German in 1936. Carlebach was taken to a concentration camp and died in a mass murder in 1942.

---

a. Copyright the Nobel Foundation; used by permission.
b. R. Yosef Tzvi Carlebach, *Das Buch Koheleth. Ein Deutungsversuch* (Frankfurt am Main: Hermon, 1936). Translated from the Hebrew translation by Prof. Miriam Gillis-Carlebach, appearing in Cohn, pp. 279–81, and presented with the permission of the translator.

It seems that anyone who has delved at one time or another into our Bible is repeatedly pulled, as if by magic cords, to the book of enigmas, to Ecclesiastes. What is it that this great king from Jerusalem wanted to share with us, this king so aware of human life, who experienced so intensely the full gamut of human agony and joy? Does this book really bespeak surrender, submission and despair in determining its awful verdict: "all is vapor and agony"? Is Ecclesiastes really the book of pessimism and lack of faith, a book which casts doubt on all human values?

...There are two kinds of pessimism: the pessimism of self-destruction, on one hand, and the pessimism of liberation, on the other hand. The first makes even the smallest moment of happiness bitter and loathsome, while the second grants us independence, unshackles us and dulls the sting of life's disappointments, no matter how great they be.

The Book of Ecclesiastes is of the second type and it comes to teach: do not imagine yourself to be the special victim of fate. Do not overestimate your suffering, for the blows of fate are an integral part of human existence.

Human life rises or falls only out of full recognition of lack of any certainty. One cannot plan by depending on continuity, on absolutes, or on logic when it comes to human life and its problems. If our lives progressed as we would want – if the waves of destiny carried us along serenely and securely – there would be no question of optimism or pessimism. It is only in light of complex and self-contradictory developments as time goes by that the tearing question of the meaning of life arises, the problem of the import and significance of the individual. It is therefore all the more important properly to evaluate developments and not to give in or to give up, in spite of failures. We tend to exaggerate in evaluating details, and do not recognize their true import. For that reason one must honestly face the naked truth in order not to be shattered by its power.

Ecclesiastes is the book of opaque happiness of life, happiness which knows of the tragedy of existence. It is the book of humility – the humility of a man who knows neither self-glorification nor conceit. This book comes to tell you that you should not take delight in wealth or possessions, praise or honors, success or power. Do not equate your life with material values. The essence of life is beyond life, in God and His commandments.

Happiness may be found in any given moment, but with no guarantee that it will continue and with no claim to its possession – quite the opposite: true happiness is inherently rooted in its unstable and impermanent quality. Joy itself is desirable and good only when it fills our hearts – but with reservations. It is specifically when facing death that such a moment becomes the source of happiness which does not disappoint.

Only if you let yourself understand the ways of the world, their eternal cycles, their superficiality and their relativity will this be a comfort to you. If you see life as it really is, only then will it be impossible to take from you the joy of the moment.

Therefore, Ecclesiastes is not a book of false optimism, it is not a narcotic which is followed by the shock of awakening, it is not a book of deception and failed memory, but it is the book of the Sage with his eyes in his head who accepts the arrival of happiness with gratitude, a gift from fate. As to his suffering, he bears it with equanimity for he knows: suffering is not his exclusive portion....

This Sage leads us through all the stages of life, which is to say: as long as one's self remains the center of everything, life's totality will remain disappointing, and one can even come to hate life. But if one directs his gaze at the wide world in its variations and in its swinging motion – up-and-down, back-and-forth – he will learn that no man is alone in his catastrophe. All are brothers in sorrow.

Then death arrives – that greatest guide to life.... It is specifically death that teaches us how valuable is every small moment in which we can do something good – "Act today, that is the way." Seize the hour – for it will not return. Fill the immediate present hour with happiness – before it disappears to never return, before the plagues of old age and death fall upon you and stop you from acting.

From the depths of seriousness, death grants the soul its freedom, and it rises and soars above all the skepticism of human existence, and death gives the soul the wings to ascend to the way of God and His commandments.

Haim Shapira: "Life Unadorned and Undisguised"[a]

It was the philosopher Simone Weil who noted that the overwhelming anger of all the pessimistic philosophers both against quickly approaching death and against the suffering in life has no logical basis – if life is vapor and suffering, why protest against death which redeems us from its hardships, once and forever?

The poet of this scroll is not one of those philosophers. He hates death because of his strong love of life. Kohelet loves life and hates it at one and the same time – he loves life because it is magnificent, and he hates life because it is vapor, anguish, and a passing shadow.

I am not a great enthusiast of the optimistic approach to life. At the basis of this optimism lies pure terror. I humbly submit that this uncritical optimism derives first and foremost from fear of the truth. The optimist is not willing to look life and death straight in the eye.

Because Kohelet is brave, he cannot be an optimist; because Kohelet is wise, he cannot be a pessimist – Kohelet sees and describes life unadorned and undisguised, honestly and movingly.

a. Haim Shapira, *Ecclesiastes: The Biblical Philosopher* [in Hebrew] (Or Yehuda, Israel: Kinneret, Zmora-Bitan, Dvir, 2011), p. 223. Used by permission.

Yitzhak Ogen: "Kohelet"[a]

Translation: Peretz Rodman and Benjamin Segal

His smile is like a golden fruit
Seen 'twixt the lips of what he says.
Pine-scented shade on hot dry days,
Benevolence, goodness are his suit.
In the heat of all that is yea-and-nay,
Negating the expected and the desired,
And I kneel (as commanded) glassy-eyed,
At the well that the living does betray –
He speaks to me and kisses my thought
With an ancient parable. His word:
The autumn simplicity conferred,
And he no celebration sought.
His wisdom is painful
Yet health and redemption its thread;
How advantageous your struggle – Vapor of vapors,
Kohelet said.

a. Yitzhak Ogen, *Hahar veha'ilan* [Hebrew, The mountain and the tree] (Tel Aviv: Eked, 1977), p. 20. Translation printed with the permission of the publisher.

Ya'akov Fichman: "Kohelet"[a]

Translation: Peretz Rodman

Of many evils, worst is to be foolish.
Of virtues, best of all is to be wise.
One wisdom did I miss, though, being mulish:
To love without a wherefore or a why.
To love, and not to cling to what's mere raiment
Or foolishness that boasts in proud display.
For love has no reward, it has no payment,
'cept flourishing that's hidden deep away.
And so my store of melancholy grew,
With barks and howls my cistern filled by turns.
For naught were all the riches, all the fame.
I learned that we can straighten what's askew!
With heart that flutters, flares, and loses flame –
For wisdom? No! For flowering it yearns.

Binyamin Galai: "A Generation on Earth"[b]

Translation: Peretz Rodman

Meaningless, said Kohelet.
Meaningless, it's all meaningless.
What comes of all a person's suffering
under the sun?
A generation is born and dies, and the earth
Does not stumble.
These are the words of Kohelet, and all the rest
is but a vapor of vapors.

a. Yaakov Fichman, *Kitvei Yaakov Fichman, 1881–1958* [Hebrew, Writings of Yaakov Fichman, 1881–1958] (Tel Aviv: Dvir, 1959), p. 38. Translation printed with the permission of the publisher.
b. Binyamin Galai, *Shirim aharonim, 1990–1995* [Hebrew, Last poems, 1990–1995] (Tel Aviv: Zmora-Bitan Dvir, 1996), p. 29. Translation printed with the permission of the publisher.

Lea Goldberg: "Poems of the Journey's End"[a]

Translation: Rachel Tzvia Back

Editor's introduction: Reflected here is also a rabbinic midrash [interpretative statement] that King Solomon wrote the Song of Songs as a youth, Proverbs when he was older than that, and Ecclesiastes as an old man.

1.

The path is so lovely – said the boy.
The path is so hard – said the lad.
The path is so long – said the man.
The grandfather sat on the side of the path to rest.
Sunset paints his grey head gold and red,
the grass glows at his feet in the evening dew,
above him the day's last bird sings
– Will you remember how lovely, how hard, how long was the path?

2.

You said: Day chases day and night – night.
In your heart you said: Now the time has come.
You see evenings and mornings visit your window,
and you say: There is nothing new under the sun.
Now with the days, you have whitened and aged
your days numbered and tenfold dearer,
and you know: Every day is the last under the sun,
and you know: Every day is new under the sun.

3.

Teach me, my God, to bless and to pray
over the withered leaf's secret, the ready fruit's grace,
over this freedom: to see, to feel, to breathe,
to know, to hope, to fail.
Teach my lips blessing and song of praise
when your days are renewed morning and night,
lest my day be today like all the yesterdays,
lest my day be for me an unthinking haze.

a. Lea Goldberg, first published, *Dvar hapoelet* [Hebrew, The word of the working woman], 4, nos. 2–3 (1954). English from *Lea Goldberg's Selected Poetry and Drama* (Jerusalem: Toby Press, 2005); reprinted by permission of the publisher.

Yehuda Amichai: "A Man in His Life"[a]

Translation: Chana Bloch

A man doesn't have time in his life
to have time for everything.
He doesn't have time enough to have
a season for every purpose. Ecclesiastes
was wrong about that.
A man needs to love and to hate at the same moment,
to laugh and cry with the same eyes,
with the same hands to throw stones and to gather them,
to make love in war and war in love.
And to hate and forgive and remember and forget,
to arrange and confuse, to eat and to digest
what history
takes years and years to do.
A man doesn't have time.
When he loses he seeks, when he finds
he forgets, when he forgets he loves, when he loves
he begins to forget.
And his soul is seasoned, his soul
is very professional.
Only his body remains forever
an amateur. It tries and it misses,
gets muddled, doesn't learn a thing,
drunk and blind in its pleasures
and in its pains.
He will die as figs die in autumn,
shriveled and full of himself and sweet,
the leaves growing dry on the ground,
the bare branches already pointing to the place
where there's time for everything.

a. Hebrew original in *Sha'at chesed* [Hebrew: Time of grace] (Tel Aviv: Schocken, 1982), pp. 50–51. English from Chana Bloch and Stephen Mitchell, eds., *The Selected Poetry of Yehuda Amichai* (Berkeley: University of California Press, 2013). Reprinted by permission of the translator.

8. Twenty Questions for Discussion

In the recent past, many publishers of novels have seen fit to append questions for further thought, perhaps in anticipation of discussions in book clubs or other organizations. Partially because this commentary sees Ecclesiastes as a "narrative" or "tale," I list here a number of (randomly ordered) questions as possible starting points for discussions based on this commentary.

1. Given that the narrator expressed a different point of view from Kohelet in the last verses, how can one explain that he wanted the book to be read, and, given his disagreements, do you think that was reasonable?

2. The commentary suggests that Kohelet had no children. Do you think that having a family might have, or would have, changed his perspective?

3. Some commentators hold that Kohelet did not pursue activities to help the unfortunate, an analysis that partially reflects the silence of the text, but possibly also partially suggests a conviction that such activities grant life the very meaning that Kohelet did not discover. Was Kohelet, then, looking for meaning in the wrong place?

4. It has been suggested that the later practice among some Jews of reading Ecclesiastes on the holiday of Sukkot [Tabernacles] is a critique of sorts, since that holiday finds meaning specifically in the impermanent, namely in the *sukkah* (booth), which becomes the center of activity for the week. Moreover, the Bible implies that one can choose to be joyful on that holiday, not just wait for joy to arrive. Is there an inherent tension between the holiday and the book?

5. This commentary suggests that Kohelet hoped for enjoyment, but that "happiness" was not on his horizon. Do you think that the terms are

different? How so? How would you define what Kohelet sought (and what you seek)?

6. An exercise: In 3:1–8, Kohelet describes alternating patterns of life. Are there dualities from your personal life that you might add? (Members of a discussion group might be asked to write down their answers, then to be discussed by the group.)

7. At the end of the Review Essays, this commentary explains that it does not use the terms "pessimism" and "optimism." Do you think that either could be applied to Kohelet or to the book, and if so, how? Has your own willingness to use these terms changed in light of reading Ecclesiastes?

8. In the same section, this commentary prefers to summarize Ecclesiastes as seeing the world as "incomprehensible" rather than as "absurd." Would you choose one term or the other, or some third term? Do you associate with either description?

9. Several selections, particularly the poems in the section Literary Reactions to Ecclesiastes, seem sharply critical of Kohelet, and perhaps of the whole work. Are you? Do you find yourself in sympathy with or for Kohelet?

10. Quoted in that same section, the poet Wislawa Szymborska calls Kohelet one of the greatest poets and yet sharply disagrees with him. Compare that to your reaction to the book.

11. This commentary suggests that as Kohelet got older he became less critical of traditional norms. Do you see this as a positive or a negative development?

12. Recalling that the implied author of Ecclesiastes is neither Kohelet nor the narrator, do you think that the author could have been a woman?

13. If you can imagine both devout religionists and atheists appreciating Ecclesiastes, how so, and if not, why not?

14. Traditional Jewish literature, in attributing this book to Solomon, claimed that he wrote it at the end of his life. Could this book have been written by a young person?

15. Would you say that Kohelet was more critical of his fellow human beings or of God?

16. Would you use the term "religious" to describe the character Kohelet?

17. Do you think that Ecclesiastes belongs in the Bible?

18. At what age should one first read Ecclesiastes?

19. This commentary suggests that some of the changes in Kohelet's attitudes and positions might be attributed to his getting older and closer to death. To what degree would you also attribute these changes to his searching for truth by observing others (part II) as opposed to only his own life experience (part I)?

20. In some Jewish congregations Ecclesiastes is read annually. Does the value of the content justify that practice?

The interested reader might also return to the citations that opened this volume, and relate to each, now that the book has been read and studied.

Research and Reference Notes

1. Temper Longman III, *Fictional Akkadian Autobiography* (Winona Lake: Eisenbrauns, 1991), argues that Ecclesiastes reflects the genre of fictional autobiography (as noted by Seow, p. 119).

2. This is noted by Cohn, p. 236. (but he does not relate it to 1:2 and 12:8).

3. A "generation" as a time period is noted in Graham Ogden, "The Interpretation of *dor* in Ecclesiastes 1:4," *Journal for the Study of the Old Testament* 34 (1986): 91–92, and Whybray, NCB, pp. 40–41. In addition to Ogden's arguments, I note that the text splits and adds to a known two-word phrase ("generation and generation"), which always refers to a time period. (For similar splits of two-word phrases, cf. "faithfulness and steadfastness," Ps. 57:11; 108:5; "resident and alien," Ps. 39:13).

4. Based on Whybray's (NCB, p. 39) discomfort with the usual translation, "all things are wearisome." He suggests reference to this root as "hard [continuous] labor." Alternatively, "wearisome" could be used if the verse is emended, assuming that a doubled letter fell out – reading *meyagim* for *yegaim* (contra Gordis, who holds that one may translate that way without emendation).

5. Following Ibn Ezra and many moderns.

6. The Midrash shows awareness of the Genesis background, as noted by Cohn, p. 221. In *Kohelet Rabbah* 1:2, R. Yehuda ben R. Simon focuses on the "seven" appearances of "vapor" (a creative view based on three uses of the singular "vapor" and two of plural "vapors") of 1:2 as reflecting the first seven days. The Midrash, however, does not reflect the tension between the two books.

7. Thus commentators hold antithetical interpretations: Crenshaw, p. 64, sees verse 1:6 as reflecting "being caught in a rut," whereas Whybray (OTG, p. 41ff.), suggests that it implies a dependable universe.

8. Verses 1:13; 2:3; 3:1.

9. "Coffers" – following NJPS, based on mishnaic Hebrew, according to Rashbam, Sforno, Kara, and others. Many interpreters relate this unique term to the root meaning "breasts" and translate "many concubines" (as in NRSV).

10. This phrase contradicts other biblical views that memory of the righteous (not the wicked) lasts – cf. Proverbs 10:7; Psalm 112:6.

11. "Anxiety" includes the same Hebrew *ra'ayon*, found in two cases of *ra'ayon ruach* (1:17; 4:16), that phrase almost universally taken as the equivalent of *re'ut ruach*, "anguish." The

combination with heart is unique, usually translated by context (e.g., NJPS, "worrying"; NRSV, "strain"; NIV, "anxious striving").

12. As Murphy points out, citing A.G. Wright, but there is no reason to assume that our author did not create the poem. (For said approach, see J. Blensikopp, "Ecclesiastes 3:1–5: Another Interpretation," JSOT 66 (1995): 54–64, but see rejection in Rudman, pp. 83–86.)

13. Longman, p. 36.

14. Some theologically slanted commentaries tend to find in Ecclesiastes "the earliest Old Testament document to express…the thought that there is something beyond death" (Ogden, p. 15). The text does not support that claim.

15. Whybray (NCB, p. 75), correctly notes that this conclusion is not based on a close inspection of Kohelet's use of the term, but on the general tone of the book. However, the conclusion still holds.

16. See Barton, p. 115.

17. Following Saadiah Gaon.

18. The present translation is a variation based on Gordis's translation (in turn, based on Ibn Ezra, even though Gordis lists this only as a possible interpretation, calling the verse an "insuperable crux"), though unlike Gordis I take "land" to indicate a small, not large, division (as in Gen. 23:15, dealing with ownership).

19. Following NJPS, NRSV, NIV, and most commentaries. "Him" is missing in the Hebrew text and must either be assumed or the text emended, ma'anehu for ma'aneh.

20. Contra Gordis.

21. This phrase in the Hebrew would seem to refer to the man, making no logical sense. I follow several medieval commentators as well as Murphy, Crenshaw, NJPS, and others in applying it to the stillbirth.

22. Kruger claims that 7:1–12 represent "problematic pieces of advice," which Kohelet rejects, and Seow sees these as a "parody." Both approaches suffer from the drive for literal consistency, and neither appreciates the complexity of Kohelet or his thought. The literary presentation "who can tell what is best?" followed by advice of what is "best" is not meant to dismiss the latter, but rather to emphasize the hesitance and tenuousness.

23. Whybray, NCB, p. 112.

24. Cf. 9:7; 11:9; Proverbs 15:15; Esther 1:10; 5:9.

25. See Ingram, pp. 172–75, for the many commentators who understand that this phrase is parallel to "enjoy" (s-m-ch).

26. As per Gordis, citing rabbinic Hebrew.

27. "Ten" is probably a large round number, as opposed to any specific reference to a standing institution (according to Saadia Gaon, Rashbam). Whybray (NCB, p. 122), cites an apt parallel, "Am I not more to you than ten sons?" (1 Sam. 1:8).

28. As pointed out by Arnold Ehrlich (late nineteenth–early twentieth century), cited by Fox on this verse.

29. Literally, "word" or "thing" (davar), a root appearing five times in these five verses (as Seow points out). Verse 8:1 might be read (as in Ibn Ezra), "Who is like the wise man, and who [is like he who] knows the interpretation of a thing!" a praise of wisdom, with the

rest of the verse noting the advantage of wisdom. As translated here, the "saying" refers to the second half of the verse.

30. I follow the pronounced as opposed to the written text, as preferred by NJPS, NRSV, NIV, and others.

31. Following W. Hertzberg, cited by Gordis.

32. Reading *bet* for *kaph*, as per the Targum and most modern commentators.

33. This may be a phrase of foreign origin, common enough to have been understood in antiquity – an Egyptian text predating Kohelet seems to refer to finding bread that had been tossed on the water. See Nili Samet, "The Gilgamesh Epic and the Book of Kohelet," *Biblica* 96, no. 3 (2015): 375.

34. See for example Barton and Gordis. Kruger calls it a "collage."

35. See Seow, p. 381.

36. Noted by Bin-nun, pp. 18–20.

37. Understanding the Hebrew *vechatuv* as *vechatov*, a gerund (as in NJPS, Gordis, others), which requires only the change of a diacritical mark.

38. Perhaps implies "intensive relearning" or "scrutinizing" rather than writing – see Nachum Bronznik, "Making of Many Books" [in Hebrew], *Beit Hamikra* 25 (1980): 213–18, based on early rabbinic Hebrew.

39. "As the judges say after they have heard all the evidence: 'This is the verdict'" – following Ramban (Nachmanides), "Exposition on Ecclesiastes" [in Hebrew], *Torat Chayim*, 19.

40. Following Gordis, Barton, and many others.

41. Several commentaries separate out verses 13–14 (or just 13b–14) as a later addition. However, even Fox, who does so, admits that such a postscript would not contradict the epilogue, and the indications of separate authorship fall far short of proof. The epilogue is best read as a unity (as in Barton, Gordis, Scott, and others).

42. Within modern literary theory, one school of thought (Reader Response Theory) holds (and I simplify) that the text in and of itself says little or nothing – what the reader finds in the text is the only reality that matters. Even within that school, however, some claim some objective content in the text. For a summary in terms of Ecclesiastes, see Salyer, pp. 52–53.

43. "Too many passages in the book could only have been written by a nonroyal person (4:1–3; 5:7–8; 8:2–6)." Longman, p. 30.

44. Longman, p. 66.

45. Fox, p. 4.

46. Readers interested in the phenomenon should consult "pseudepigrapha" in any encyclopedia. There are entire books so written included in various "Holy Scriptures" of other religions, and some attribute sections of the Hebrew Bible to this category as well.

47. A possible reflection of Kohelet's childlessness can be found by comparing the text to a section in the Gilgamesh epic (tablet 10, column 3), an ancient text that prefigures some of Ecclesiastes: "You, Gilgamesh, let your belly be full. Keep enjoying yourself day and night. Every day make merry; dance and play day and night! Let your cloth be clean. Let your head be washed, may you be bathed in water! Gaze on the little one who holds your hand! Let a wife enjoy your repeated embrace! Such is the destiny [of mortal men]."

Translation according to Andrew George, *The Babylonian Gilgamesh Epic* (Oxford: Oxford University Press, 2003), pp. 278–79. Gilgamesh includes children in the prescription for happiness, whereas Ecclesiastes does not.

48. Bickerman, p. 154.

49. Note the speech of Polish poet Wislawa Szyborska, 1996 Nobel Laureate for Literature: "I sometimes dream of situations that can't possibly come true. I audaciously imagine, for example, that I get a chance to chat with the Ecclesiastes..." whom she so admires, and then goes on to challenge him. That sentiment is repeated in many reactions to Ecclesiastes.

50. The assumption that the author of Ecclesiastes intends to convince readers of a single point of view continues to haunt commentators. Salyer, p. 12, summarizes the use of a first-person narrative as a "rhetorical gamble that backfires," in that it makes the "claim" less well based. Had the purpose been to convince, then the point might be valid, but that is not the case.

51. See my book, *A New Psalm: The Psalms as Literature* (Jerusalem: Gefen Publishing and Schechter Institute of Jewish Studies, 2013), pp. 13–15.

52. Salyer, p. 165ff.

53. See Ingram, p. 127, for a chart of the appearances of the term in the book.

54. See summary, Christianson, p. 194.

55. As pointed out by Christianson, pp. 220–21. See verses 1:3; 3:9; 5:15; 6:8, 11. (This is limited to the [rhetorical] question. Kohelet continues to discuss specific advantages – 7:12; 10:10, 11.)

56. Christianson, ibid. There are six uses of "who" from verse 6:12 on, only one use before. The quotes in this sentence are from Christianson.

57. 7:6, 24, 26; 8:13; 9:8, 12; 10:1, 8ff.; 11:1, 5; 12:1–7, 11. The clear early uses, apart from "vapor," are "hastens" ("pants for," 1:5), and the "three-ply cord" (4:12). I do not relate here to "dead" or "stock" metaphors (such as "heart," "darkness," and probably "sweet" in 5:11), but only to those that were possibly original. That said, the question of identifying metaphors being complex, we must await more research before determining final lists.

58. In this understanding, 3:16–17 would express dismay at no such existence, followed by a hope ("I said in my heart") that it would exist; 4:1; 7:15; and 8:11–12a would then bemoan examples of its absence, but 8:12b–13 would express confidence in ultimate justice, with 8:14 attributing the problems to *temporary* confusion; while 11:9 would include a restatement of an expected application of justice. This reading, however, is uncertain.

59. "It is clear that Koheleth does not present a systematic philosophy." Gordis, p. 128.

60. Fox, p. 3.

61. Miller, pp. 163–67. Both Fox and Miller reflect inspiration from Brueggemann's schema of Psalms: orientation, disorientation, and reorientation. Walter Brueggemann, *The Message of Psalms* (Minneapolis: Augsburg, 1984).

62. Christianson, pp. 227–50.

63. Cohn, p. 272ff., emphasizes that much later advice in the book relates to what one should not do.

64. In fact, later in his work Fox rephrases what he earlier called "building up": "These are not solutions but *accommodations*.... They allow humans to find good things – *little meanings* – within the vast absurd" (p. 140, emphasis in the original).

65. "Ecclesiastes...invites the reader to think for himself" (Whybray, OTG, p. 13, but the book is not as exceptional in the biblical landscape as Whybray believes). Note also Shapira, p. 222: "The text of this book invites the readers to think for themselves about the issues that occupy this wise poet.... Ecclesiastes sends us on individual searches for one's way within the Valley of the great questions."

66. Isolated Christian commentators sometimes lose sight of this emphasis and see the book as confused or incomplete, e.g., Longman, p. 284: "Jesus...is the ultimate answer to Qohelet's conclusion of meaninglessness under the sun."

67. See note 42.

68. I would claim that one traditional Jewish approach to sacred text is precisely that one may dialogue with it in different ways at different times in one's life. (These comments should not be confused with any claim that Ecclesiastes itself is best approached through a "postmodern" or "deconstructive" reading. It is not.)

69. Kruger, p. 18.

70. The apocryphal *Ecclesiasticus* (see 49:10), c. 190 BCE, suggests an awareness of all of Prophets. See below on the date of Ecclesiastes. Since the Septuagint, many Bibles have interspersed the Prophets and the Writings to some degree, and it is not universally agreed that the division in the Hebrew Bible reflects the stages of canonization. Nevertheless, the division does reflect very different types of literature, which is basic to this inquiry.

71. Included, however, are some historical records, especially Ezra, Nehemiah, and Chronicles, as well as a number of historical tales based in history but scarcely chronicles: Ruth, Esther, and Daniel.

72. See also *Eduyot* 5:3.

73. *Shabbat* 30b, which cites internal contradictions. See also Tosefta, *Yadaim* 2:14, which attributes the content to Solomon, not God, and *Pesikta de Rav Kahana* 8, and *Vayikra Rabbah* 28:1, which cite possible apostasy.

74. Shimon ben Shetach, 40–12 BCE, in J. *Brachot* 7b.

75. As emphasized by Gurevitch, pp. 31–35.

76. For detailed references, see Gordis, p. 364n10.

77. Several commentators attribute that purpose to the epilogue, as an addition to the book.

78. *Shabbat* 30b.

79. Gordis, p. 43.

80. Christianson – see the bibliography. I do not accept all of Christianson's interpretations, particularly concerning the meaning of the word "vapor" (for him, "absurdity"), nor do I accept his insistence that the pose of Solomon is maintained (to a degree) throughout the book.

81. Definitions taken from Christianson, pp. 11, 21; the quoted definition cited from G. Prince, *Narratology: The Form and Functioning of Narrative* (Berlin: Mouton, 1982), p. 1.

82. Note particularly Salyer, pp. 83–85, who prefers "argument" to "narrative." Some of his objections to "narrative" are well based (including the absence of "causality"), but the claim for "argument" is much less so.

83. Sometimes these attempts are so obscure that they testify primarily to the commentator's need for a title, not to the nature of the work, as in Longman's "framed wisdom autobiography," p. 17.

84. Bickerman, p. 157.

85. There are a number of studies of Ecclesiastes that proceed on the unstated assumption that the book was written to make an argument as opposed to sharing observations, a claim not found anywhere in the book. Some then come to unusual conclusions, such as the "poor method" chosen to make the argument or the "inconsistency" of the presented system, when neither implied goal was there in the first place.

86. For one example, see Gordis: "The language and style of Koheleth represent the latest stage in the development of Hebrew to be found in the Bible and the closest approximation to Mishnaic Hebrew" (p. 59), and "The abundance of Aramaisms in Koheleth is precisely what we should expect in the work of a Hebrew writer of the Second Temple period" (p. 61).

87. Of late, Seow has proposed an earlier date for Ecclesiastes, in the early fourth century BCE. See, however, Rudman's summary of Seow's approach and Rudman's successful defense of the mid–third century date (chapter 1, and pp. 146–48).

88. For more detailed treatment, see Gordis, pp. 51–58; Kruger, pp. 73ff., 112, 122. Rudman has a particularly intensive and detailed exploration, pp. 173–99. He finds "'significant parallels" and "some kind of connection" to Stoicism, but concludes, "Qoheleth is not a Stoic" (pp. 198–99). Sneed is absolute in his denial: "There is no definitive and clear evidence of Greek ideas or values in Qohelet" (p. 131).

89. For striking examples, see Barton's citation of a section from Gilgamesh, p. 162, part of which is quoted above in note 47 (including, by way of paraphrase, "since the gods declared death for man … you should fill your belly, day and night being joyful"); an ancient Akkadian text ("Who can understand the counsel of the gods in the midst of heaven?," ANET, p. 435, "I Will Praise the Lord of Wisdom"); and Fox, p. 12, citing an Egyptian text of the fourteenth century BCE: "A generation passes, another stays, since the time of the ancestors.… Yet those who build tombs, their places are gone. What has become of them?" That last cited text goes on to recommend a life of joy. Further on Gilgamesh, see Nili Samet, "The Gilgamesh Epic and the Book of Kohelet: A New Look," Biblica 96, no. 3 (2015): 375–90.

90. Bickerman, p. 154, citing one exception – Proverbs 24:32.

91. Cohn, p. 225, holds that while the perspective of all other books of the Bible is theocentric, Ecclesiastes is anthropocentric.

92. Bickerman, p. 154ff.

93. Ibid., p. 150.

94. Fox was a pioneer in this regard. Others who build on the variety of voices include Perry and Bin-nun. The recognition of potentially different voices is much older, however, and is cited by Ibn Ezra on 7:3. The list of voices that follows is longer than other lists.

95. I use the singular for convenience – it could be a group effort. In fact, the first to identify the framework as an alternate author was Rashbam, who uses the plural at the end of the book. The one singular usage, "*my* son" (12:12) is a commonplace in Wisdom literature and need not imply one writer.

96. Rashbam implies on 1:2 that the narrator "organized" the text. In EM, p. 74, Fox argues that the frequent use of first person ("I said," "I said to my heart," etc.), especially in places of movement from one subject to another, best fits the assumption that Kohelet assembled his own statements.

97. This is one of the most repeated contentions concerning the epilogue, as reflected in the heading in Barton: "12:9–12 – A Late Editor's Praise of Qoheleth and of Hebrew Wisdom, to Which Is Added a Chasid's Last Gloss (12:13–14)." Whybray (NCB, on this verse) insists on two authors, and mentions the possibility of a third.

98. Rashbam, commenting on 12:8, although he uses the singular in a parallel statement on 1:2.

99. See Murphy, pp. 125–30, for one such approach.

100. According to Fox, pp. 367–69, who also cites eight other ancient pieces of literature that use this technique.

101. Fox, pp. 361 and 144, respectively. Similarly, Seow, p. 38, is willing only to say that these verses are probably from a different hand.

102. Fox, pp. 144, 361. Also note, "Modern scholars are divided on the authenticity of this section as an original part of the Book.... Driver... asserts, 'There does not appear to be any sufficient reason for doubting that 12:9–12 is by the author of the Book....'" Cohen, p. 189.

103. Salyer, p. 50, summarizes R. Barthes's theory as follows: "Written language swallows up the author upon publication of a work, creating the 'death of an author.'"

104. See Salyer's summary, pp. 63–66, basically meaning the author as reflected in the work.

105. The Talmudic rabbis discussed de-canonizing Ecclesiastes because Kohelet's words are self-contradictory (*Shabbat* 30b). Ibn Ezra lists nine sample contradictions in his comments on verse 7:3, noting that there are more.

106. Ibn Ezra on 7:3.

107. For an extended explication of this method, see Gordis, pp. 95–108. Evidently, Rashbam was the first to claim that certain verses or parts thereof were quotations.

108. Principally, J.A. Loader, *Polar Structures in the Book of Qohelet* (Berlin: DeGruyter, 1979). This approach has not gained significant acceptance.

109. This is the approach of Perry in his commentary.

110. This is the approach of Bin-nun and Medan. The two approaches cited in this subparagraph date back at least to the Church Father and translator of the Bible, Jerome (fourth century CE), but have had only isolated support since then.

111. For fuller treatment, see Fox, pp. 1–4, and Miller, p. 158ff.

112. Salyer, pp. 400–402 (my calculation).

113. Fox, p. 16ff. On pp. 14–26, Fox surveys various suggestions reflected in the typology above and rejects them all.

114. In Mann's essay on Freud, delivered October 16, 1929, cited in Shapira, p. 32.

115. This is the approach of Fox, who related directly to the suggested "incomprehensibility," rejecting the term because he thinks that it implies that there is an explanation beyond human ken. The use of "incomprehensibility," however, does no such thing. It simply implies that human reason cannot fathom the phenomenon, without implying that there is an explanation that exists elsewhere. Fox, pp. 33–35.

116. As in Fox, p. 3: "Qoheleth is not so much contradicting himself as *observing* contradictions in the real world."

117. Gordis, p. 88.

118. "…this is a deliberate technique adopted by the author." Ingram, p. 37. Ingram's thesis is that ambiguity is the hallmark of Ecclesiastes.

119. The "author has consciously constructed a text which would recreate the same sense of *hebel* at a literary level that one experiences in real life." Salyer, p. 17ff.

120. Compare Ronald Benun's suggestion that the alphabetic order of Psalm 10 is purposely interrupted for as long as the text talks about evil disrupting the world: "Evil and the Disruption of Order: A Structural Analysis of the Acrostics in the First Book of Psalms," *Journal of Hebrew Scriptures* 6 (2006): 5.

121. Rashbam.

122. Ibn Ezra.

123. Ezra 2:55–57 and Nehemiah 7:57, 59, where the two terms, as professions, would indicate "writer" and "catcher of gazelles."

124. Ingram, p. 84ff., citing Iain Provan. This seems to be a far-fetched proposal.

125. Sforno constantly emphasizes this differentiation.

126. Bin-nun and Medan. The four personalities identified are the pleasure seeker, the worker, the wise man, and the God-fearer, and the commentary presents two separate suggested attributions of the verses among these four personalities, but these two often differ one from the other.

127. Perry.

128. Ibn Ezra on this verse.

129. Gurevitch, pp. 32–34.

130. There are forty uses that are metaphoric. (See Miller, pp. 190–93, for a full list.) Some of the biblical applications of the metaphor are not used in Ecclesiastes, including "idolatry" and "immorality."

131. Christianson, p. 80.

132. Uncertain – it was written in the fourth or third century BCE. See my *Song of Songs: A Woman in Love*, pp. 49–50.

133. Christianson, pp. 80–81.

134. This is particularly true of commentaries, wherein an author can comment at length, as opposed to freestanding translations, where only the text will be available to readers. Even in the latter case, this option is seldom to be preferred.

135. Miller – see the bibliography. This being the subject of the entire book, I do not indicate page references in the coming paragraph. One can find a summary in his introductory chapter.

136. Miller offers a fourth category of his own, "symbol," which is close enough to the single-metaphor category to be included therein.

137. One can cite the example of Scott, who uses the following terms (and others!): breath, vapor, futile, empty, hollow, transitory, meaningless, and fleeting.

138. Fox, p. 36, where he continues, "or failing that, to a great majority of them," an unnecessary choice, as I indicate below.

139. Fox, p. 30.

140. The last is a relatively recent suggestion. Shields, pp. 119–21.

141. Fox on this verse.

142. "In *almost* all cases, it means 'absurd.'" Fox, p. 35 (my emphasis). "A word is needed that best represents the majority of the instances." Christianson, p. 87.

143. Fox, p. 87, quoting Camus.

144. In rejecting "absurdity," Sneed comments, "Qohelet's main message is *human limitation*. . . . His concern is primarily anthropology, not theology" (p. 162).

145. Fox, p. 34.

146. Fox was influenced by his sense of the book as reflecting Camus rather than his understanding of the terminology, as he confesses: "Since 'absurd' in common usage has connotations of the ludicrous, in a translation of popular use another gloss, such as 'senseless,' might be more appropriate. In this book I prefer 'absurd' because of its associations with a philosophical tradition that I consider akin to Qoheleth's thought" (p. 31n5).

147. Miller – see his summary, pp. 92–97, and the charts, pp. 181–85. He finds each use to relate to one, two, or all three of the qualities, sometimes implying "futile" or "disgusting."

148. Christianson counts 75 percent of the uses of the term in chapters 1–6.

149. Most interpreters equate the two phrases when *ra'ayon* is used with *ruach*, but translate in an ad hoc manner for the one use of *ra'ayon lev* (*lev* means heart), verse 2:22.

150. In terms of root meanings, the issues have remained the same for more than a hundred years. See Barton, pp. 85–86, for a summary.

151. The Targum and the Vulgate ("vexation of spirit"), Saadia Gaon ("twisting of the soul"), and Rashi (approximately, "heartache").

152. Schoors summarizes: "as an adjective, denotes the painful or unfortunate aspect of a situation, as a substantive . . . damage or harm; in sum, all sorts of evil in the broadest sense. It is seldom used for moral evil" (p. 152). *Rasha* is the term for moral evil, translated here as "wicked."

153. Gordis, pp. 93ff., 227ff., citing earlier interpretations. The root maintains its alternative implication of "sin" in verses 7:20 and 8:12, though the context clarifies that implication, and so the translation "failure" is maintained for the sake of unity.

154. See Ginsberg, p. 10, for the Aramaic origin of this usage.

155. Kruger: "someone who, without personal effort, is granted the favor of the Godhead" (p. 72). Schoors writes, "It is clear that in Qohelet *tov* [good] never refers to an absolute good but always means 'good for the human being'" (p. 44). Also see Gordis, p. 91.

156. Seow, pp. 104–6. (He thinks that "under the heavens" may not be an exact equivalent to "under the sun," but rather indicates the physical differentiation as opposed to the temporal one.)

157. Contra Cohn, who writes, p. 243: "[Kohelet] hints at a superior world…a world above the sun, a spiritual and ethical world where there is no vapor." One may integrate such personal beliefs with Kohelet's, but Kohelet himself neither says nor hints at it. If anything, toward the end he may include anything after death also in the category "vapor" (11:8).

158. Longman, p. 66.

159. Ibid.

160. Sforno constantly emphasizes this differentiation, but in contradistinction to true reward and punishment in a more understandable world, which does exist elsewhere. Ecclesiastes, however, does not in any way imply that alternative or deal with it.

161. The "literal" school of translation – see Edward Greenstein, "Theories of Modern Biblical Translation," *Prooftexts* 3, no. 1 (January 1983): 10.

162. "There is perhaps no other book in the Hebrew Bible that has such relentless individualism." Christianson, p. 34.

163. I hope that I have addressed Christianson's comment that accompanies his listing of all occurrences of "I": "Most of these occurrences cannot be properly represented in English and the major translations duly ignore them" (p. 39).

164. Addison G. Wright, "The Riddle of the Sphinx: The Structure of the Book of Qoheleth," *Catholic Biblical Quarterly* 30, no. 3 (July 1968) and subsequent articles. (Most rejections of his system were based on a noncorrelation between the proposed division and the units of meaning.)

165. Ogden, p. 11, lists eight failed efforts over a period of decades. I see these as reflective of an instinct that "feels" structure, even if it has been hard to find.

166. Verses 3:10–15 can be seen as the first of seven sections in part II (see the commentary, part I, section 3, especially p. 35 note a). If so, it would not have a "core term" (a phrase I define in the following paragraphs) unless one considered all the uses of '-*s'h* ("create," make," "do," etc.) in Part I as part of the count, in which case, the plurality of uses would appear there.

167. Already termed a "refrain" by Ginsberg, p. 5n3.

168. Based on the understanding that experiencing "the good [life]" is the linguistic equivalent of experiencing enjoyment – see commentary and Ingram, pp. 172–75.

169. See, in particular, F. Rousseau, "Structure de Qohelet i-4-11 et plan du livre," *Vetus Testamentum* 31 (1981): 200–217.

170. See the rejection of Rousseau in Whybray, OTG, p. 44. Whybray is seeking "a comprehensive development of thought" (p. 45).

171. Any reader interested in pursuing this subject must not rely on my brief summary. In terms of the included bibliography, Salyer and Ingram were most influenced by these schools of thought, and one should refer to those works and to the literature cited.

172. Ingram, p. 18, part of a summary of the approach of Wolfgang Iser.

173. Quoting Ingram, p. 1.

174. The body of Ingram's work pointedly analyses six "ambiguities." Of these, one is an oft-used metaphor (vapor) that is inherently ambiguous; one is the name Kohelet (and names are often punned with multiple "derivations" in the Bible); one is a new term ("advantage"), which may just be an attempt to coin a new philosophic term; two are ambiguous only when compared to their earlier uses in the Bible ("toil" and "good"); and one ("under the sun") may not be ambiguous at all. Even given these explanations, however, the six may contribute to an "air" of ambiguity – and as to an evaluation thereof, see below.

175. Perry, p. 3.

176. Scott, p. 193.

177. "Qohelet is no existentialist in the modern sense.... Qohelet never goes so far as Camus in proclaiming the world to be absurd." Sneed, p. 168.

178. Gordis, p. 129.

179. Note Whybray's (OTG, p. 12) range, citing two commentators. The first: "The book asserts that life is profitless, totally absurd.... The world is meaningless. Virtue does not bring reward. The deity stands distant, abandoning humanity to chance and death." The second: "The book's theme is that life under God must be taken and enjoyed in all its mystery." Note also the titles of two articles on Ecclesiastes: "The Optimism of Qohelet" and "The Pessimism of Ecclesiastes." Ingram, pp. 44–49, surveys the wide variety of overviews.

180. This phraseology is borrowed from Abraham Joshua Heschel, *Israel: An Echo of Eternity* (New York: Farrar, Straus and Giroux, 1969), used there to describe the return of the Jews to the Land of Israel in terms of systems of Jewish thought.

Bibliographical References

The following are titles that are referenced in the footnotes and research notes either by the name of the author(s) or by the brief title as noted here. Texts cited less often are referenced with full information in the notes. Full bibliographies of studies on Ecclesiastes are available in the various commentaries and in biblical dictionaries and encyclopedias. Inclusion in the present list does not imply a recommendation.

Barton, George Aaron. *A Critical and Exegetical Commentary of the Book of Ecclesiastes*. Edinburgh: Clark, 1908.

Bickerman, Elias. "Philosophy of an Acquisitive Society." In *Four Strange Books of the Bible*, 139–69. New York: Schocken Books, 1967.

Bin-nun, Yoel, and Yaakov Medan. *I Am Kohelet: A Chorus of Voices in a Single Persona* [in Hebrew]. Alon Shevut: Alon Shevut, 2012.

Christianson, Eric S. *A Time to Tell: Narrative Strategies in Ecclesiastes*. JSOT Supplement Series 280. Sheffield, UK: Sheffield Academic Press, 1998.

Cohen, A., ed. *The Five Megilloth*. London: Soncino, 1946.

Cohn, Gabriel. "Ecclesiastes." In *Studies from the Five Scrolls* [in Hebrew], 217–90. Jerusalem: Ministry of Education and Culture, 1984.

Crenshaw, James L. *Ecclesiastes: A Commentary*. London: SCM Press, 1988.

Encyclopedia Mikra'it (EM) [The biblical encyclopedia], s.v. "Kohelet" (Ecclesiastes), by Michael V. Fox, vol. 7, col. 70–83. Jerusalem: Bialik Institute, 1976.

Fox, Michael V. *A Time to Tear Down and a Time to Build Up*. Grand Rapids, MI: Eerdmans, 1999.

Ginsberg, H. Louis. *Studies in Kohelet*. New York: Jewish Theological Seminary of America, 1950.

Gordis, Robert. *Kohelet the Man and His World: A Study of Ecclesiastes*. New York: Schocken, 1968.

Gurevitch, Zali. *Kohelet's Account* [in Hebrew]. Tel Aviv: Bavel, 2008.

The Holy Bible: New International Version (**NIV**). Grand Rapids, MI: Zondervan, 1989.

Ibn Ezra, Avraham [b. Spain, wandered, d. France, 1167]. Text (Hebrew) as in Katzenelbogen, *Torat Chayim*, in this bibliography.

Ingram, Doug. *Ambiguity in Ecclesiastes*. New York and London: Clark, 2006.

Isaiah of Trani [Italy, thirteenth century – attributed to one of two who bore this name, grandfather and grandson]. Text (Hebrew) as in Katzenelbogen, *Torat Chayim*, in this bibliography (there listed as the Elder).

Jewish Publication Society. *Tanakh: The Holy Scriptures* (**NJPS**). Philadelphia: Jewish Publication Society, 1988.

Kara, Joseph [France, late eleventh century]. Text (Hebrew) published in *R. Josef Kara und sein Kommentar zu Kohelet*. Berlin, 1886.

Katzenelbogen, M.L., ed. *Torat Chayim: Kohelet, with Early Commentaries* [in Hebrew]. Jerusalem: Mosad Harav Kook, n.d.

Kruger, Thomas. *Qoheleth: A Commentary*. Minneapolis: Augsberg, 2004.

Loader, J.A. *Polar Structures in the Book of Qohelet*. Berlin: DeGruyter, 1979.

Longman, Temper, III. *The Book of Ecclesiastes*. New International Commentary on the Old Testament. Grand Rapids, MI: Eerdmans, 1998.

Miller, Douglas B. *Symbol and Rhetoric in Ecclesiastes: The Place of* Hebel *in Qohelet's Work*. Leiden: Brill, 2002.

Murphy, Roland E. *Ecclesiastes*. World Bible Commentary. Dallas: World Books, 1992.

National Council of Churches. *The Holy Bible: New Revised Standard Version* (**NRSV**). Grand Rapids, MI: Zondervan, 1989.

Ogden, Graham. *Qoheleth*. Sheffield, UK: Sheffield Academic Press, 1987.

Perry, T.A. *Dialogues with Kohelet: The Book of Ecclesiastes; Translation and Commentary*. University Park: Pennsylvania State University Press, 1993.

Pritchard, James, ed. *Ancient Near Eastern Texts Related to the Old Testament* (**ANET**). 2nd ed. Princeton: Princeton University Press, 1975.

Rashbam [France, c. 1082–1105], *The Commentary of R. Samuel ben Meir (Rashbam) on Qoheleth* [in Hebrew]. Edited by Sara Japhet and Robert B. Salters. Jerusalem: Magnes Press, 1985.

Rashi [France, 1040–1105]. Text (Hebrew) as in Katzenelbogen, *Torat Chayim*, in this bibliography.

Rudman, Dominic. *Determinism in the Book of Ecclesiastes*. JSOT Supplement Series 316. Sheffield, UK: Sheffield Academic Press, 2001.

Saadia Gaon [Baghdad, d. 942]. Text (Hebrew) as in Katzenelbogen, *Torat Chayim*, in this bibliography.

Salyer, Gary D. *Vain Rhetoric: Private Insight and Public Debate in Ecclesiastes*. JSOT Supplement Series 327. Sheffield, UK; Sheffield University Press, 2001.

Scott, R.B.Y. *Proverbs and Ecclesiastes. The Anchor Bible*, vol. 18. New York: Doubleday, 1965.

Schoors, Antoon. *The Preacher Sought to Find Pleasing Words: A Study of the Language of Qoheleth*. Part II, Vocabulary. Belgium: Peeters, 2004.

Seow, C.L. *Ecclesiastes: A New Translation with Introduction and Commentary. The Anchor Bible*, vol. 18C. New York: Doubleday, 1997.

Sforno, Obadiah [Italy, d. 1550]. Text (Hebrew) as in Katzenelbogen, *Torat Chayim*, in this bibliography.

Shapira, Haim. *Ecclesiastes: The Biblical Philosopher* [in Hebrew]. Or Yehuda, Israel: Kinneret, Zmora-Bitan, Dvir, 2011.

Shields, Martin A. *The End of Wisdom: A Reappraisal of the Historical and Canonical Function of Ecclesiastes*. Winona Lake, IN: Eisenbrauns, 2006.

Sneed, Mark R. *The Politics of Pessimism in Ecclesiastes*. Atlanta: Society of Biblical Literature, 2012.

Whybray, R.N. *Ecclesiastes*. Old Testament Guides. Sheffield, UK: Sheffield Academic Press, 1989. Referenced as "Whybray OTG."

Whybray, R.N. *Ecclesiastes*. New Century Bible Commentary. Grand Rapids, MI: Eerdmans, 1989. Referenced as "Whybray NCB."

Wright, Addison G. "The Riddle of the Sphynx: The Structure of the Book of Qoheleth." CBQ 30, no. 3 (July 1968): 313–34, with follow-up articles CBQ 42 (1908): 38–51; CBQ 45 (1983): 32–43.